THE OLD CHINA TRADE

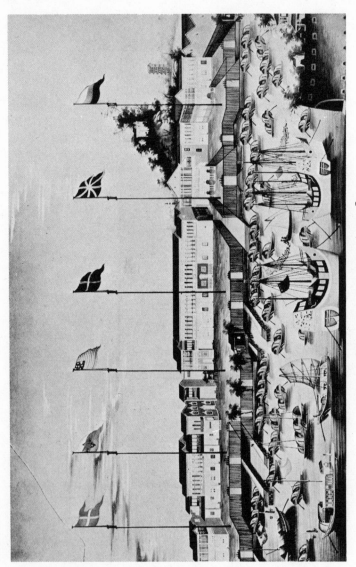

THE CANTON FACTORIES BEFORE 1821

# THE OLD CHINA TRADE

BY

FOSTER RHEA DULLES

WITH ILLUSTRATIONS

AMS PRESS
NEW YORK

Reprinted from the edition of 1930, Boston
First AMS EDITION published 1970
Manufactured in the United States of America


Library of Congress Catalog Card Number: 70-111470
SBN: 404-02216-2

AMS PRESS, INC.
New York, N. Y. 10003

# PREFACE

In this story of the old China trade I have attempted to recapture something of the spirit of adventure and daring which at the close of the Revolution sent the young merchant seamen of the Atlantic seaboard throughout the length and breadth of the Pacific. Many of these voyages had as their objective other ports than Canton, but it was the China trade which gave greatest proof of the resourcefulness and ingenuity of the Yankee traders. Furthermore, it had a significant result in the opening-up of political relations with the Chinese Empire. I have brought the story to a close with the Treaty of Wanghia, which was signed in 1844. It ushered in a new era in our trade with China; it also brought to an end its most romantic period.

The text has not been burdened with footnotes, but the reader interested in knowing the sources on which I have based my work is referred to the list of official documents, manuscripts, contemporary articles, and books which I have consulted and found useful. This list, needless to say, makes no pretense of being a complete bibliography.

To the officials and librarians of the New York Public Library, the New York Historical Society, the New York Society Library, the Essex Institute, and the Peabody Museum I should like to extend my most sincere thanks. I am also indebted to Mrs. Helen Godey Wilson for letting me see manuscripts in her possession, to Dr. Howard C. Taylor, Jr., for many suggestions, and to Marion R. Dulles for so much help and encouragement that her name might better be inscribed as that of a collaborator.

F. R. D.

New York, *January*, 1930

# CONTENTS

# ILLUSTRATIONS

# THE OLD CHINA TRADE

.. ..

## CHAPTER I

### THE EMPRESS OF CHINA

THE ink was hardly dry on the treaty which marked England's acceptance of American independence when the merchant seamen of the young republic were scouring the seven seas in search of trade. At home all was confusion. The ineffectual Congress established under the Articles of Confederation was trying in vain to bring some order out of the chaos resulting from the rivalries and jealousies of thirteen independent governments; industry, trade, and farming were almost at a standstill; depreciated currency was bringing in its train both wild extravagance and bitter poverty, and in Massachusetts the agrarian revolt which was to culminate in Shays's Rebellion was raising its ugly head. Yet out of this turmoil and disunity the American merchant marine was born.

One of the markets first sought in the spectacular expansion of our commerce after 1783 was that of Canton. With the old trade routes which had absorbed the bulk of colonial trade now closed to them, the merchants of the Atlantic seaboard had to look far afield. They could no longer carry American products to Spain or Africa, bring back slaves to the West Indies, and from there import rum, sugar, and molasses. England had no intention of allowing an independent America to monopolize so lucrative a commerce with her still faithful colonies. New ports had to be discovered and new trade routes developed to replace those on which

the colonials had been so dependent. Otherwise political
independence might well prove a barren victory. This was
the challenge which was met by the first long voyages to
the Far East.

It mattered little to adventurous seamen, who had won
their salt-water spurs in the privateers of Revolutionary
days, that they knew nothing of the waters beyond the Cape
of Good Hope. Without either charts or proper nautical instruments to guide them to their distant goal, in ships so
small that to-day they would scarcely venture outside a
harbor, they were soon finding their way through the Indian
Ocean and beating up the China coast with the southwest
monsoon.

The year in which George Washington was elected the
first President of the United States saw fifteen American
vessels lading teas and silks from the musty godowns at
Canton. Ships from New York, Boston, Philadelphia, and
Salem, which a few years before had been preying upon
English commerce in the Atlantic, were already boldly cutting into the trade hitherto monopolized by the great East
India Company. Chinese merchants and American supercargoes had found a basis of mutual confidence and friendship which was to mean fortunes for them both.

Another half-dozen years and these American ships with
their young and vigorous crews were not only perfectly at
home at Mauritius, Batavia, Calcutta, and Bombay, but
were skirting the rugged coast of Northwest America to
trade with the Indians and hunting the fur seal on the barren islands about Cape Horn. All the Pacific was theirs.
By the opening of the nineteenth century they were regularly freighting 'Eastern goods to Europe as well as to
America, carrying on a contraband trade in the Spanish
ports of South America with copies of the Declaration of

Independence scattered in their wake, and discovering new islands in the South Seas.

This commerce with the Oriental and other ports of the Pacific cannot be fitted into neat categories and statistically analyzed. The Yankee seamen followed the fortunes of trade as an adventurer might follow the fortunes of war. Rounding the Cape of Good Hope, they perhaps would try to dispose of their cargo at Mauritius and take freight to Canton for the French merchants of that thriving island, or they might trade in cotton at Bombay and Calcutta, pepper in Sumatra, or sugar and coffee at the Dutch port of Batavia. If they had rounded Cape Horn there was smuggling on the California coast, barter with the Northwest Indians, or trade wherever they could find it in the southern Pacific. The homeward voyage might be direct, it might mean stops at any European port from Hamburg to Leghorn.

Nevertheless, it was in Canton that this early trade in the Pacific reached its peak. This distant port, where the hong merchants trafficked in Bohea, Souchong, and Hyson, sold the finest silks of the East for Spanish dollars, and exchanged their nankeens and chinaware for furs and ginseng, was the ultimate goal which most of the first traders sought. It was to gratify the rich tastes of luxury-loving mandarins that American seamen braved the perils of Nootka Sound and the Seal Islands in their hunt for furs, or felt their way through the treacherous shoals of the South Sea Islands in the quest for sandalwood and *bêche de mer*. The old China trade, shrouded in mystery and romance to those who remained at home, has been with good reason a symbol for the initiative and daring which characterized the commerce of its day.

But it is not only that in the voyages to the Far East there was being written a story of adventurous achievement which forms the brightest chapter in the maritime history of the United States. It is not only that they gave to American commerce the impetus which enabled it to overcome the economic stagnation of the Revolution and resulted in American ships becoming the common carriers of the world during the Napoleonic wars. These voyages were a new expression of the pioneer spirit which was to carry America's frontiers steadily westward until the way to the Pacific lay open by land as well as by sea. They revealed new horizons to a people hitherto narrowly restricted to the activities permitted them by the mother country. They helped to give to the United States a new confidence in its destiny.

The honor of dispatching the first voyage to Canton fell to New York. On the initiative of Robert Morris, financier of the Revolution, a 360-ton privateer renamed the *Empress of China* sailed from this port for the Far East the year after the treaty of peace. Its owners hoped, as Morris wrote to John Jay, 'to encourage others in the adventurous pursuit of commerce.' [1]

Canton was chosen as the goal of this voyage because it was the world's great market for tea. In this age and generation tea may not seem an important enough commodity to be responsible for an entirely new commercial development. We think of foreign trade in terms of steel, rubber, oil, cotton, and the hundred and one products of an industrial age which may range from locomotives to electric light

[1] If this was the first mercantile voyage from the United States to the Far East it is nevertheless a curious fact that a century earlier American pirates had found their way around the Cape of Good Hope. In 1698 the Earl of Bellomont, Governor of New York, wrote in a report to the Lords of Trade and Plantations: 'I find that those Pyrates that have given the greatest disturbance in the East Indies and Red Sea have either been fitted from New York or Rhode Island, and manned from New York.'

bulbs. But at the close of the eighteenth century there were few of these things even in existence. What this country sought, in exchange for its own exports of breadstuffs, tobacco, rice, wood, and fish, were cotton and woolen manufactures, wine and spirits, molasses, sugar, coffee and tea. If a voyage to the East meant a cargo of Hyson and Bohea free of all English duties, with some silks, nankeens, and chinaware thrown in, it was well worth whatever effort it involved.

America had always had to rely upon England for its tea. The East India Company had an absolute monopoly on English trade at Canton and its imports were reshipped from England to the Colonies. But at the close of the Revolution, tea was one product on which the people of the new nation were especially loath to pay further tribute to the British Treasury. Had there not been some years before a rather memorable tea-party in Boston Harbor?

To exchange for the teas of China the Americans had one commodity in which they had great hopes. This was ginseng, a root used by the Chinese for its supposed miraculous healing qualities. It grew wild both in Manchuria and in the forests of the New World and was a drug so marvelous in the eyes of the Chinese that the Emperor had made its cultivation in the remote mountains of his empire an imperial monopoly. Known as the 'dose for immortality,' it was worth its weight in gold. At various times, when it threatened to become extinct in China, the Emperor had forbidden its collection except for the imperial household and as a high reward would confer the drug upon officials whose health had broken down.[1]

[1] Whatever value ginseng had for the Chinese was purely psychic. The root itself shows no evidence of any pharmacological or therapeutic properties. It was forked and in the shape of a man, and so supposed to restore virile power to the aged and infirm.

The ginseng which grew in the United States was of an inferior quality to that grown in China, but it was known that it commanded a high price in the markets of Canton. How this discovery was first made is a complete mystery. Yet, by the middle of the eighteenth century, agents of the East India Company had identified American ginseng and it was being collected for export to England, whence it was reshipped by the Company to Canton.

Whiskey and trinkets were offered to the Indians on generous terms for gathering the precious root, and throughout New England and New York the woods were searched by bands of men, women, and children. It was a traffic which occasioned that worthy divine Jonathan Edwards great distress. The Indians spent their time in the woods, to 'the neglect of public worship and their husbandry.' And even sadder, as we find him writing in 1752, they took the ginseng roots to Albany, where they invariably found themselves 'much in the way of temptation and drunkenness.'

The bulk of the cargo of the *Empress of China* was consequently made up of ginseng. It carried 473 piculs, or about thirty tons of the drug.[1] Other articles assembled by Robert Morris and his associates, the New York firm of Daniel Parker and Company, included 2600 fur skins, 1270 camlets, 316 piculs of cotton, 476 piculs of lead, and 26 piculs of pepper. The total investment in the voyage was $120,000.

For such a hazardous venture as a first voyage to Canton, it was natural that the care applied to assembling a suitable cargo should also be extended to the equipment of the vessel and the selection of its crew. The guns and armament of the *Empress of China* were not disturbed, for they might prove useful as protection against the pirates which were

[1] A picul was the Chinese 'hundredweight,' generally equal to 133⅓ lb. avoirdupois.

known to infest Eastern seas, and as captain of the vessel a man with experience in the privateers of Revolutionary days was selected, Captain John Green. The crew itself was made up of four officers including Captain Green, a surgeon and his mate, a purser, two midshipmen, and a clerk; and before the mast thirty-four men including a gunner, two carpenters, a cooper, and several boys.

For supercargo, the man charged with the mercantile business of the voyage and protection of the owners' interests, Robert Morris had chosen Samuel Shaw, and for his assistant, Thomas Randall. Shaw was a young Bostonian who had left the counting-house to serve with distinction throughout the Revolution, becoming aide-de-camp to General Knox. A testimonial from Washington declared that he had 'distinguished himself in every thing which could entitle him to the character of an intelligent, active and brave officer.' Beyond that the judgment and business capacity he had shown as General Knox's aide had attracted wide notice. Morris and his associates could not have chosen a better man to inaugurate their trade with China, while for Shaw it represented an opportunity to win his way back into the mercantile world. On December 24, 1783, he wrote his brother of his plans to sail to the East — 'the terms on which I go promise something clever, and I hope to shake you by the hand in two years.'

In his new rôle he was to display all those qualities for which he had been recommended by Washington and Knox. Shrewd, far-sighted, and of keen judgment, he was well equipped to deal with the merchants of Canton, but even more important, his tact and understanding were the qualities most necessary to win their friendship both for himself and for the country he represented. Samuel Shaw was not destined to live long enough to give full expression to his undoubted abilities, but the service he performed in opening the China trade should serve to keep his memory alive.

One other thing was done before the vessel sailed. Daniel Parker wrote to Congress requesting a sea letter for Captain Green. This important document, duly signed by the president and secretary of Congress, was grandiloquently addressed to the 'most Serene, most Puissant, High, Illustrious, Noble, Honorable, Venerable, Wise and Prudent, Lords, Emperors, Kings, Republicks, Princes, Dukes, Earls, Barons, Lords, Burgomasters, Councillors, as also Judges, Officers, Justicians, and Regents of all the good cities and places, whether ecclesiastical or secular, who shall see these patents or hear them read.' Congress was taking no chances in its first address to the mysterious potentates of the East.

When all was at last in order the *Empress of China* set forth on its 13,000-mile voyage. It was Washington's fifty-second birthday, February 22, 1784. 'In passing the grand battery,' Shaw wrote in the journal[1] he kept of the enterprise, 'we saluted with thirteen guns, and received twelve in return.'

The vessel's first stop was at the Cape Verde Islands. Here fresh water and supplies were obtained, and Shaw records that the sailors bought a 'little green monkey with a black face.' Then after everything had been made shipshape they started on the long and leisurely passage about the Cape of Good Hope and across the torrid waters of the Indian Ocean. Five months out of New York they at last sighted Java Head, which was to become such an important

[1] Shaw's journal, the first and the most extensive account of the trade at Canton, was edited with a life of the author by Joseph Quincy, under the title 'The Journals of Major Samuel Shaw, the first American Consul at Canton,' Boston, 1847.

Samuel Shaw

Amasa Delano

Benjamin Morrell

Richard Cleveland

FOUR MERCHANT SEAMEN

landmark for all voyages to the Far East, and on July 18 anchored in the Straits of Sunda.

This was for all on board the *Empress of China* a first experience of the Orient. The palm-fringed shores above which rose terraced rice-fields, the vivid green of thick tropical foliage, the land breeze laden with the scent of strange exotic spices, must have made Java a delightful apparition to seamen who knew no ports other than those of the Atlantic. Soon several canoes put off from the shore, and the sailors were buying fowls, cocoanuts, turtles, and fruit from dark-skinned Malays in batik loincloths and turbans. For half a dollar they bought as many fish as would serve both cabins for supper.

Shaw and the officers went ashore to visit the settlement at Serigny. They were met by a chief attended by more than a hundred of his countrymen armed with spears and knives. 'Me grandee Bantam,' this imposing official introduced himself, and cordially invited the Americans to enter his house. 'There was something noble and very pleasing in his looks,' the journal notes, 'while his behavior was altogether friendly and engaging.'

But more important, the Americans found in the Straits of Sunda two French ships also bound for Canton. These representatives of their country's former ally greeted them in the most friendly way and insisted that the *Empress of China* accompany them on the difficult and dangerous passage which lay ahead. This Captain Green was only too glad to do, and for a month the three vessels kept together until they reached the Portuguese port of Macao, outpost of Canton, where all foreign ships had to obtain permission from the mandarins, or Government officials, to proceed up-river to the Chinese port.

It was August 28, after a voyage of almost half a year,

when this first American ship to find its way to the Pacific reached the Canton anchorage at Whampoa. Here the *Empress of China* proudly saluted the foreign shipping with thirteen guns and dropped its anchors. Immediately, officers from the French, English, Dutch, and Danish vessels in port boarded the newcomer to welcome the American flag to this distant part of the world.

All of the Europeans were surprisingly cordial. If the French took it especially upon themselves to initiate the Americans into the intricacies of the Canton trade, the representatives of the other nations were no less friendly. This included the English. 'It was impossible to avoid speaking of the late war,' Shaw wrote. 'They allowed it to have been a great mistake on the part of their nation, — were happy it was over, — glad to see us in this part of the world, — hoped all prejudice would be laid aside, — and added, that, let England and America be united, they might bid defiance to all the world.'

Among the Chinese the Americans were regarded as the 'New People,' and Shaw took great pains to explain the extent of the country from which he came and the possibilities of trade which his initial venture opened up. The attitude he took toward the Chinese and the impression he made upon them were of great importance to his successors. Consequently there is more than passing significance in this conversation with a Chinese merchant as it is given in his journal:

'"You are not Englishman?" said he. "No." "But you speak English word, and when you first come, I no can tell difference; but now I understand very well. When I speak Englishman his price, he say, 'So much, — take it, — let alone.' I tell him, 'No, my friend, I give you so much.' He look at me, — 'Go to hell, you damned rascal; what!

you come here, — set a price my goods?' Truly, Massa
Typan, I see very well you no hap Englishman. All China-
man very much love your country."

'Thus far, it may be supposed,' continues Shaw, 'the
fellow's remarks pleased me. Justice obliges me to add his
conclusion: — "All men come first time China very good
gentlemen, all same you. I think two three time more you
come Canton, you make all same Englishman too."'

In their four months' stay at Canton under such favorable conditions, the Americans had no difficulty in disposing
of the cargo of the *Empress of China*. In a report of the
Select Committee of the East India Company to its Court
of Directors, it was stated that the American vessel's
return lading consisted of 2460 piculs of black tea, 562
piculs of green tea, 24 piculs of nankeens, 962 piculs of
chinaware, 490 pieces of silk, and 21 piculs of cassia. In
addition to this, the assistant supercargo, Thomas Randall,
remained after the *Empress of China* had sailed to charter
a second vessel, the *Pallas*, and followed Shaw home with
an additional cargo of tea.

The homeward voyage of the *Empress of China* began
on December 28. After a brief stop at the Cape of Good
Hope, a quick passage was made across the Atlantic, and on
May 11, 1785, the vessel was brought to anchor 'in the East
River at New York, when we saluted the city with thirteen
guns, and finished our voyage.'

Within a few days there appeared in the New York
papers among their notices of runaway slaves and of
auctions of likely Negro wenches, an advertisement that
Constable Rucker and Company had for sale an assortment
of India goods brought direct from Canton by the *Empress
of China*: teas, chinaware, silks, muslins, and nankeens. The
'Independent Journal' spoke proudly of this 'judicious,

eminently distinguished, and very prosperous achievement.'
The 'New York Packett,' in recalling that in an earlier age
the arrival of a vessel after so prosperous a voyage and from
so distant a part of the globe would have been announced
by public thanksgiving and ringing of bells, enthusiastically
demanded: 'Should not this be our practice now, since
Providence is countenancing our navigation to this new
world?'

# CHAPTER II

## OLD CANTON

At the close of the eighteenth century, Canton was the one Chinese port open to the Western world. It had been first visited by the Portuguese in 1516. One hundred and eight years later came the Dutch [1] and in 1637 the English. An important trade had been established, but from the day on which the 'red-haired barbarians' had first arrived and, 'by their tremendously loud guns, shook the place far and near,' the Chinese had looked upon the newcomers with suspicion. Secure in their arrogant conviction that in China alone could be found any true civilization, the haughty mandarins tolerated the foreigners with studied indifference. They were permitted to trade as the princes of neighboring states were permitted to pay tribute. It was a privilege for which the nations of the Western Ocean should ever be thankful to the august clemency of the Son of Heaven.

Again and again had the Europeans attempted to break through this wall of pride and ignorance. It was absolutely impossible. Nothing could shake the celestial confidence in China as the one great nation under the blue canopy of Heaven, and in the Emperor as the lawgiver of all the world. The embassies which Portugal and Holland had dispatched to Peking could make no dent upon this feeling of self-sufficiency. Their protestations of friendship were taken as a matter of course, their presents condescendingly accepted as evidence of true humility, and their requests for

[1] A Chinese record of the arrival of the Dutch: 'Their clothes and their hair were red; their bodies tall; they had blue eyes, sunk deep in their heads. Their feet were one cubit and two tenths long; and they frightened the people by their strange appearance.'

further trading privileges indifferently waved aside. On each occasion the foreign embassies returned to Canton with empty hands.

Every imperial edict concerning the 'foreign devils' heaped scorn upon their heads. 'As the dispositions of these said foreigners are depraved by the education and customs of countries beyond the bounds of civilization,' read one of them, 'they are incapable of following right reason; their characters are formed; their perverse obstinacy is untameable; and they are dead to the influence of our renovating laws and manners.' Yet so valuable were the teas and silks of Canton that the Europeans tamely submitted to every affront offered them by the mandarins. In other parts of the East they had dispossessed the native rulers. England controlled the dying empire of the Moguls and the Dutch had made themselves lords of the East Indies, but in Canton they traded on sufferance and clung tenaciously to the few privileges which had been granted them.

The Americans quickly enrolled themselves in the submissive foreign settlement outside the city walls, and perhaps their experiences may best present a picture of actual conditions at Canton. Samuel Shaw has left us a description of the port as he found it in 1784 and later traders have somewhat added to it. It was several decades before any material change occurred. No breach was made in the impenetrable wall which China had set up against foreign encroachments until, goaded beyond endurance, the English fell back upon force and proved that in this respect at least the Chinese had to admit Western superiority.

The American vessels approached Canton from the south, as had the *Empress of China*, making their way up the China coast in the fall. At Macao, as we have seen,

they were obliged to get a *chop*, or official permit, to enter
Chinese territory, and also to take on Chinese pilots. Then
again all ships were examined at the mouth of the Pearl
River, where the forbidding Bogue forts afforded the
Chinese a somewhat questionable protection against invasion, since their guns, firmly anchored in stone sockets,
could shoot in only one direction. If all still went well, the
mandarins thereupon permitted them to proceed to the
anchorage at Whampoa, some twelve miles below Canton
itself.

Here in the winter months when the teas and silks were
in the market might be found the foreign fleet. It was always an imposing sight. Traveler after traveler bears witness to the sudden thrill he felt upon rounding a narrow
bend in the river and finding anchored in the reaches a line
of great ships which sometimes stretched for three miles.
Even in 1784 this fleet totaled forty-five vessels, and as
the trade grew and more and more American ships came
every season to take up their anchorage at the head of the
line, the number rose to well over one hundred. When
David Abeel, one of the first two American missionaries to
China, arrived in Canton in 1829 and found the East India
Company's fleet at Whampoa, he wrote enthusiastically
that it represented 'an array of naval magnificence un-
equaled in any other port.'

This was but a first introduction to the exotic charms
of Canton. When the 'fast boats' which plied between
Whampoa and Canton were taken up-river, there was spread
out before the eyes of visitors such a scene as their imagina-
tions could never have painted. The river was crowded
with Chinese shipping, strange craft of every possible
description. Great, ungainly salt junks and six hundred-
ton vessels for the Java trade lined the banks or made their

way slowly downstream, their high sterns fantastically
decorated and their sharp prows painted with huge eyes to
spy out the devils of the sea. River junks were manned by
gangs of naked coolies who treaded paddle wheels, or, like
the Christian slaves of Roman galleys, pulled on long
sweeps. Mandarin boats flying white and vermilion flags,
with red sashes tied about the muzzles of their cannons,
patrolled the shores.

Even more strange and foreign to the eyes of travelers
from the other side of the world were the gaily decorated
flower boats where the mandarins dallied with Chinese
ladies of pleasure. At night when the din of warning gongs
had subsided and the flares of burning joss paper had
died down, these craft became mysterious and disturbing.
Weird strains of Oriental music floated out over the still
river.

Nearer the city the press of boats was even thicker. In
and out among the larger vessels sped tiny sampans which
served not only as carrier boats and loaded and unloaded
the cargoes of the seagoing junks, but housed the great
floating population of the Chinese city. They were 'mysteriously abundant...everywhere they congregate in vast
numbers; like a stream they advance and retire unceas-
ingly.' Thousands were moored along the river-banks in
addition to those plying their trade, and on each of them
an entire family made its home. On the stern of every
sampan burned a tiny fire over which a woman might be
cooking the evening meal. The decks were cluttered with
pots and pans and all manner of household utensils, while
slung over the sides were wicker baskets of hens and ducks.
Children, three and four perhaps to each sampan, played
about unconcernedly with wooden buoys tied to their backs.

This was the scene which the first American visitors to

Canton came upon as they were taken up the river in 1784.
Even to-day it has changed little except for the addition of
river steamers and motor launches. Thousands of Chinese
still live on the river as did their ancestors; their tiny
sampans are still 'mysteriously abundant.'

When the fast boats passed the two Chinese forts known
as Dutch Folly and French Folly and came opposite Jackass
Point, the travelers at last could see the foreign factories,[1]
the goal of the long voyage from the West. Soon the
American flag was to be added to those which waved so
proudly from the shore, but the trading-posts first established were those of England, France, Holland, Denmark,
Sweden, Spain, and Austria. They were grouped together
in a long line some three hundred feet back from the river.
Two and three stories high, with sloping roofs and neatly
whitewashed walls, we are told that they made 'a very
pretty appearance.' The godowns where chests of tea and
bales of silks were stored took up the first floors; living
quarters were on the second and third. Covered galleries
ran through the open courtyards which separated the hongs.
The most imposing of the buildings was that of the East
India Company — 'the Factory that Ensures Tranquillity' as it was rather optimistically called by the Chinese.
It had a wide veranda supported by pillars in 'princely
grandeur.'

In front of the factories was an open square which at the
time of Shaw's visit was enclosed by a rail fence, giving the
Europeans the privilege of its exclusive use. But in 1822,
when the foreign hongs burned down and were replaced by
new buildings of brick and granite 'in a neat style, but with

[1] The 'factories' — the word is practically interchangeable with 'hongs' —
were simply the residences and business places of the 'factors,' or agents, of the
various East India companies. They were not manufactories.

slight pretensions to architecture,' this space was made a free thoroughfare. The Chinese then thronged through it at all hours either to watch with insatiable curiosity the strange antics of the barbarians or to carry on the various trades of a Chinese market. It was crowded with itinerant barbers, tailors, cobblers, jugglers, and story-tellers. Peddlers hawked their wares — pickled olives, paper umbrellas, lichee nuts, or pastry — and filthy beggars cried for alms outside the foreigners' windows. Sometimes the Chinese police would clear the square by driving off peddlers and loafers with their long whips; more often it would remain so densely packed that Americans and Europeans could hardly elbow their way through the crowd.

Near the factories were some few streets which were also open to the foreigners. Thirteen Factory Street ran behind the hongs and the square was bounded by Hog Lane and Old China Street. Here innumerable Chinese shops offered a wide variety of native wares. Ivory, silks, silver and gold might be sold or exchanged, but also one could purchase bird cages, fireworks, insects, medical herbs, cats, and dogs. There were many shops for the benefit of foreign seamen. Ostensibly their wares were curios and souvenirs and they offered tea and refreshments to draw their customers; actually samshu, a fiery local wine, was the great attraction which thronged Hog Lane with sailors of all nationalities whenever ships were in port.

All in all the plot of ground to which foreigners were restricted was not more than a quarter-mile square. Here they had to remain during the winter months while cargoes were being unloaded and exchanged for teas and silks. In the summer they had to return to Macao.

All foreign trade in Canton was strictly regulated. No Chinese was allowed to do any real business with the visitors except the members of the co-hong, a body of Chinese merchants who paid for the privileged monopoly of foreign trade. The first thing which the captain or supercargo of every newly arrived vessel had to do was to secure one of these men to act as his ship's security merchant, responsible to the Chinese authorities not only for vessel and cargo, but for its crew and their good behavior. In no other way could any business be transacted. It was the hong merchant who paid all duties to the Government and who had to submit to every exaction of the officials, who openly lined their purses with arbitrary levies upon the foreign commerce. Should the hoppo, as the chief customs officer was known, or the provincial governor, demand that the customs returns show a greater revenue, there was no recourse for the hong merchant but to produce it. He passed the burden of these demands on to the foreign traders, but the process was indirect and highly simplified. They merely paid a higher price for their tea and knew that the difference between market cost and what the hong merchants charged them was a thinly disguised bribe to officialdom for the privilege of trade.

The only direct duty levied on the shipping under this system was the measurement charge which every vessel had to pay before its cargo could be unloaded. The hoppo performed the task of determining the amount to be contributed to the Imperial Treasury and his path had to be smoothed by small bribes in the form of European curios. Clocks, watches, musical snuffboxes, and 'smellum water' were the conventional gifts. Upon the occasion of the arrival of the *Empress of China* ignorance of this custom had left Shaw without any of these articles. But he appears to have met the situation successfully. For after the ship had been measured, the hoppo sent aboard as a present to the newcomers 'two bulls, eight bags of flour, and seven jars of country wine.'

While the foreigners had to rely upon the co-hong for all trade, another such organization had been formed to handle their ships' supplies and the needs of their factories ashore. Its members were known as 'compradors,' and every vessel had to have one if it expected to take on any provisions. All other business which involved contact with the Chinese had to be performed through still a third group of specially privileged men. They supplied the sampans to load and unload the ships, and as they acted generally as interpreters — for none of the foreigners during this early period had the slightest knowledge of Chinese — they were known as 'linguists.' It was a ludicrous misnomer. None of them really spoke any foreign language and the sole medium of communication between the Chinese and their visitors was that queer jargon known as 'pidgin English.' [1]

On the whole, this unique system of trade worked well. Eventually it broke down, but in 1784 the Americans accepted it gladly. They put themselves entirely in the hands of the Chinese, and from the time of Shaw's first contact with the co-hong until the end of the period with which we are concerned — which also marked the end of the co-hong — there were few complaints on the part of American merchants. As soon as he had experienced its workings, Shaw wrote that the trade at Canton 'appears to be as little embarrassed, and is, perhaps, as simple as any in the known world.'

His testimony was corroborated by almost all his successors. To take but two examples. In 1830, an American

---

[1] The word 'pidgin,' typical of the jargon it is used to describe, was the Chinese rendering of 'business.' The dialect is largely made up of English words, used more or less according to Chinese idiom, with some Portuguese and Chinese embellishments.

resident of long standing, W. W. Wood, wrote that 'the ease and expedition with which business is conducted in China renders mercantile transactions more agreeable than in any other part of the world.' Four years later, John Robert Morrison declared in his commercial guide to Canton that there was no port where trade could be carried on with such facility and regularity.

This did not mean that commerce was not subjected to many petty annoyances and that the greed and corruption of the Chinese officials did not bring many abuses in their train. But as business as a whole was entirely carried on through the hong merchants, the chief responsibility was theirs and they lived up to their obligations. Again we have Shaw's testimony, valuable not merely because he was the first American to do business in Canton, but because his opinions were never seriously disputed. 'The merchants of the co-hoang,' he wrote, 'are as respectable a set of men as are commonly found in other parts of the world... they are intelligent, exact accountants, punctual to their engagements, and, though none the worse for being well looked after, value themselves much upon maintaining a fair character. The concurrent testimony of all Europeans justifies this remark.'

In later years American opinion of the co-hong was just as favorable. 'As a body of merchants, we found them honorable and reliable in all their dealings, faithful to their contracts, and large-minded,' wrote William C. Hunter, who first sailed for China in 1824. And just sixty years after Shaw had first paid them his respects, Robert B. Forbes, one of the most prominent Americans in the China trade, stated his absolute agreement with his predecessor's conclusions.

It was in fact from this traditional integrity of the hong

merchants that the Chinese gained their reputation for unusual honesty. But early visitors to Canton never carried their encomiums this far. From the days of the visit of an English voyager who found that the ducks he bought by weight had been stuffed with pebbles, and that sad occasion when an American trader discovered that the colors of some birds he had bought for their gay plumage washed off in the rain, the knavery of the Chinese shopkeepers had become proverbial. 'No Indians we had ever visited during the Voyage was more complete in the Art of thieving than the Chinese of the lower order... they appear'd to me to be the greatest villains in the Universe' was the outspoken opinion of one American in 1792.

The smaller dealers were in fact generally looked upon as 'almost universal rogues,' and it is only too apparent that Chinese honesty is subject to the same limitations as that of any other people. Generalizations based upon the integrity of the hong merchants, who necessarily found honesty not only the best policy but one from which they could not deviate and remain members of the co-hong, created a myth no truer during the period of the old China trade than it is to-day.

In so far as the social life of the foreigners at Canton was concerned, they were subject to as strict regulations as their commerce. The hauteur and condescension which characterized China's attitude toward the West found its expression in the rules which governed all the visitors' comings and goings. 'The barbarians are like beasts,' read a Chinese maxim, 'and not to be ruled on the same principles as citizens. Were any one to attempt controlling them by the great maxims of reason, it would tend to nothing but confusion. The ancient kings well understood this, and accordingly ruled barbarians by misrule. Therefore to rule barbarians by misrule is the true and best way of ruling them.' And of course in the eyes of the Chinese all Westerners — whether English, Dutch, French, or Americans — were barbarians.

The foreign residents accordingly had no rights outside the narrow confines of their settlement. They could not enter Canton itself or wander about the countryside. On only four days of each moon were they permitted to make excursions, accompanied by one of the linguists, to the Fati flower gardens on the opposite bank of the river or to the near-by Honam Joss-House. And then, read the fifth of the eight regulations governing their conduct, they could not go in 'droves' of more than ten at a time and must return to the factories as soon as they were 'refreshed.' They could not row on the river themselves, nor could their ships 'loiter about' or 'rove about the bays at pleasure.' And finally, 'neither women, guns, spears nor arms of any kind can be brought to the Factories,' declared one order which neatly grouped arms and females as elements equally likely to disturb the tranquillity of the Celestial Empire.

Life was cabined, cribbed, confined to an impossible degree. Samuel Shaw considered the situation in which the Europeans found themselves anything but enviable, and wrote emphatically that 'considering the length of time they reside in the country, the restrictions to which they must submit, the great distance they are at from their connections, the want of society, and of almost any amusement, it must be allowed that they dearly earn their money.' Some of his successors who remained longer in Canton eventually discovered that the comforts and luxury of life in China to some degree made up for its restrictions, but at best it was tedious and monotonous except for the busy period when the teas were actually in the market. It is true that William C. Hunter could in later life recall somewhat sentimentally that no one left Canton without regret because of the novelty of the life, the social good feeling, and the facility of all dealings with the Chinese, but there is a somewhat more realistic touch in the memoirs of one of his contemporaries who speaks of his utter dreariness in pacing up and down in the square before the factories.

In time the original regulations were slightly relaxed. The foreigners organized boating clubs and held regattas on the river; they made occasional excursions in the countryside. But the hostility of the Cantonese always made such gestures toward freedom extremely hazardous.

The rule by which 'foreign devil females' were so strictly excluded was one which remained in force throughout the entire period of the old China trade. Great was the excitement some forty-five years after Shaw's visit when first an Englishman and then an American dared to make the experiment of bringing his family to the foreign settlement.

In the case of the Englishman, the president of the Select Committee of the East India Company, who combined with this offense the heinous crime of riding in a sedan chair, the result was almost open hostilities. The Chinese threatened, the English brought up guards from their ships to defend themselves, and peace and order were restored only by the lady's hurried retreat to Macao. 'Foreigners clandestinely taking foreign females to dwell in the factories at Canton, their ascending to sit in shoulder chariots (sedan chairs),' declared an emphatic reaffirmation of the old regulation hurriedly issued by the Chinese officials, 'must both be interdicted.'

Nor was the American female invasion of Canton any more successful. William H. Low, a partner in the well-known Canton house of Russell and Company, had to send his family back to Macao almost as soon as they had arrived. The Chinese authorities were prepared to stop all trade with his firm and no weapon to enforce their regulations could be more effective.

One member of this party was Low's twenty-year-old niece, whose brief visit naturally created a sensation among the American residents. Unfortunately the delightful diary she kept of her travels in the East has survived in only fragmentary form in so far as this episode is concerned. But it is apparent, in such remarks as 'You have no idea how elegantly these bachelors live here. I don't wonder they like it,' that Canton to her was a novel and exciting experience.

'Good-for-nothing creatures that they are!' was her sole comment on the Chinese, but this was inspired by the cruel order that trade would be stopped 'if one Low did not immediately remove his family to Macao.'

# CHAPTER III

## SHIPS AND CARGOES

THE successful voyage of the *Empress of China* quickened the energies of American merchants and awoke a new interest in the Orient. Its profits had not been great considering the risk its promoters had undertaken — Shaw reported that they were but $30,727 or some twenty-five per cent on the capital invested; but, far more important, the voyage had opened up an entirely new field of commerce and proved that American traders need not fear the monopoly of the East India Company in Chinese teas and silks. Within a year of the day the *Empress of China* dropped anchor at New York, five ships had set out on the trail it had ploughed through the furrows of the Eastern seas.

New York followed up its early lead in the new trade by promptly sending back the *Empress of China* on a second voyage; dispatching the ship *Hope*, Captain James Magee, and the sloop *Experiment*, Captain Stewart Dean. From Philadelphia sailed the *Canton*, Captain Truxton, and from Salem the *Grand Turk*, a vessel which under the command of Captain Ebenezer West had already been as far as the Cape of Good Hope, where it had met the *Empress of China* on its return voyage during the previous year.

Samuel Shaw did not sail this time on his old vessel, but on the *Hope*. He had turned down the offer of Robert Morris to act again as his supercargo in order to take the post of first secretary of the War Department under General Knox, but the owners of the *Hope* had persuaded him not to give up the China trade. So we find him writing his brother that he was again sailing for the East 'under such circumstances as have induced me to resign my employment in the War Office, for *I am now certain that this undertaking will answer my most sanguine expectations.*

On the return of the *Empress of China* from its first voyage, he had made a full report on conditions in Canton to Foreign Minister Jay 'for the information of the fathers of the country.' Congress duly appreciated this service and Shaw was officially informed of 'its peculiar satisfaction in the successful issue of this first effort of the citizens of America to establish a direct trade with China, which does so much honor to its undertakers and conductors.' Consequently, when he was about to return to Canton, he was *elected* consul. 'Neither salary nor perquisites are annexed to it,' wrote Jay, 'yet so distinguished a mark of confidence and esteem of the United States will naturally give you a degree of weight and respectability which the highest personal merit cannot very soon obtain from a stranger in a foreign land.' Shaw accepted the post and requested the Foreign Minister to convey to Congress 'my most humble and grateful acknowledgements for the honor they have been pleased to confer upon me.'

With vessels from New York, Philadelphia, and Salem all China-bound, Boston was the only important seaport which seemed to lag in this sudden rush to tap the markets of Canton. Yet it was only by an odd mischance that it had not been the pioneer in the whole trade. Even before the *Empress of China* had sailed from New York, the fifty-five-ton sloop *Harriet*, Captain Hallet, had set out from Hingham with a cargo of ginseng destined for Canton. Stopping at the Cape of Good Hope, however, it had met an East-Indiaman whose captain, alarmed at this Yankee threat to his company's monopoly, offered Captain Hallet double the weight of his cargo in Hyson tea. So it was that, while the *Empress of China* was crossing the Indian Ocean, the *Harriet* turned homewards. Instead of Boston's papers being able to announce a successful trip to Canton, the 'Independent Chronicle' on July 29, 1784, could only carry a brief advertisement of 'fresh teas taken out of an Indiaman and brought by Captain Hallet from the Cape of Good Hope.'

A few years, however, and a Boston vessel had not only made its way to Canton but had ventured around Cape Horn to the Northwest Coast of America and then returned around the world. The Massachusetts seaport quickly made up for its delayed start in the Oriental trade, while other early competitors to New York, Philadelphia, and Salem arose in Providence and Baltimore. The former port's first vessel for Canton sailed by way of India in 1787.

Each of these cities had some special claim to glory in the opening of the China trade. If New York really initiated it, it was Philadelphia which for several years had the greatest tonnage anchored in the reaches of Whampoa. If Boston developed the trade with the Northwest Coast and sent the first American vessel around the world, Providence started its Eastern commerce with more capital and was notable for such large ships as the nine-hundred-and-fifty-ton *President*.[1] But there is no question that it is Salem which popularly has always been most closely associated with Canton.

During the Revolution, Salem had been one of the few ports not closed by war and it had equipped and sent out to harry British shipping no less than one hundred and fifty-eight privateers and letters of marque. Peace found this great fleet lying almost idle and the discovery of new commercial

---

[1] 'She moved majestically from the Slips,' reads a contemporary account of the launching of this great vessel in 1791, 'amidst the Plaudits of an immense Concourse of Spectators, among whom was a brilliant assemblage of the fair Daughters of America.'

routes was even more important to Salem's prosperity than
to that of the other ports on the Atlantic seaboard. Elias
Hasket Derby, the port's greatest shipowner, quickly took
the initiative in expanding Salem's commerce, sending the
first American ship to St. Petersburg and the Russian ports
on the Baltic, and dispatching the *Grand Turk* first to the
Cape of Good Hope and then to Mauritius and Canton.

When in 1789, fifteen American vessels were trading with
China, five of them came from Salem, and all but one of
these five belonged to Derby. In the fifteen years which
followed the Revolution, he sent out some one hundred and
twenty-five voyages which included forty-five to the Far
East. Nevertheless, after the first few years comparatively
little of Salem's commerce continued to be with Canton
itself. Derby seems to have abandoned the China trade
altogether as early as 1790, and his successor, Joseph Peabody, made Canton the goal of only seventeen of his eighty-
seven Eastern voyages. Trade with Mauritius, the British
ports of India, and the pepper coast of Sumatra drew Salem
vessels far more than did Canton.

The explanation of why Salem still remains symbolical
of the old China trade despite these facts is that no other
port so carefully preserved the records of its commerce.
We know more of its trade in Canton than we do of the
trade of its rivals, even though Salem certainly follows New
York, Boston, and even Providence in the number of its
ships which reached the China coast.[1] We may be thankful
for that pride in the exploits of its seamen which has left to
Salem such a glorious heritage in the logs and sea journals

[1] Kenneth Scott Latourette, who has listed five hundred and twenty American voyages to Canton between 1784 and 1844 — probably not half the actual
total — gives the following figures for home ports: New York, 136; Boston, 111;
Providence, 79; Salem, 71; Philadelphia, 27; miscellaneous, 42, and unknown,
48.

of adventurous voyagers in Eastern waters, but we must recognize that other ports are fully entitled to share its fame.

Whatever the rival claims of any of these cities, however, it is enough that in the years which found the United States striving to form a centralized government and to establish its industries and commerce on a firm footing, a fleet of American vessels was annually making its way to Canton. Despite their small size, despite all the hazards of the long voyage from the Atlantic Coast, despite the inexperience of the seamen and their total ignorance of that part of the world which lay beyond the Cape of Good Hope, these ships succeeded in winning for America more than its share of China's rich trade. No longer did the people of the young republic have to rely upon England for their teas and silks and nankeens. To the consternation of British traders, who confidently had predicted that whatever direction American commerce might take, it would never infringe upon their monopoly at Canton, the products of the East were being directly imported by American merchants in American ships.

The size of these vessels is the first thing to startle our imagination in a day of mammoth ocean liners. They averaged less than three hundred tons, and many merchants unable to raise the capital to load and equip a ship of even this tonnage sent out vessels so small that their voyages seem incredible. No better example of the indomitable spirit of enterprise which made possible the development of the China trade can be found than in the story of the second trip to Canton. The *Experiment*, first of those to sail after the return of the *Empress of China*, was nothing more than a sloop of eighty tons built for trade on the Hudson River. Yet with a crew of eight men and two boys, it made the

direct voyage to the Chinese port without loss of a single
man and returned in triumph to New York some sixteen
months after it had left, warping into dock while 'martial
music and the boatswain's whistle were heard on board
with all the pomp and circumstance of war.'

Nor was this the only time when the amazed English
sailors aboard the thousand-ton East-Indiamen thought
an American ship at Canton must be the tender for some
larger vessel. Joseph Ingraham in 1792 brought in the
brigantine *Hope*, 'being only 70 tons and slightly built';
a few years later, Edmund Fanning called at Canton with
sealskins in the course of a voyage around the world in the
ninety-three-ton *Betsy*, which carried a crew of thirty, not
one of whom was over twenty-eight; and in 1807, the
*Pilgrim*, sixty-two tons, was in Canton after a voyage of
several years in the southern Pacific.

But perhaps the most amazing record for navigating
Eastern seas in small ships was that of Captain Richard
Cleveland. Born and brought up in the mercantile atmosphere of Salem, he had soon won command of one of 'King'
Derby's fleet and in 1797 found himself in France with the
barque *Enterprise*. He had intended to sail for Mocha for a
cargo of coffee, but circumstances compelled the owners to
cancel the voyage. Instead of returning to America with the
*Enterprise*, Cleveland thereupon decided to purchase a vessel himself and sail for the East on his own responsibility.

It was in a tiny thirty-eight-ton cutter that he set out
from France bound for Mauritius. When he put into the
Cape of Good Hope, the English were so astonished at the
size of the vessel that they could not believe its purpose was
legitimate trade. They concluded that the cutter was
secretly carrying dispatches for the French Government and
forced Cleveland to sell it and abandon his voyage. The

crew with which this venturesome American was prepared
to round the Cape and cross the Indian Ocean was composed of a nineteen-year-old Nantucket lad, a gigantic
Negro who had formerly been a slave, a 'great, surly,
crabbed, raw-boned, ignorant Prussian,' and a thirteen-
year-old French boy who was 'the very image of a baboon.'

On another voyage a fifty-ton cutter with a mutinous
crew of British deserters was Cleveland's command on a
daring and hazardous voyage from Canton to the Northwest Coast. When he reached Nootka Sound on Vancouver
Island, he found that even the Indian canoes were often
larger than his own vessel. Still a third voyage found him
sailing from India to Mauritius on a twenty-five-ton pilot
boat with open decks, an unheard-of feat which created
even more of a sensation at Mauritius than his previous
exploits had done at the Cape or at Canton.

There were, of course, some larger vessels in marked
contrast to these little brigantines, sloops, and cutters, but
if the scarcity of American capital put a premium on small
ships, American skill and ingenuity made their voyages
highly successful. Furthermore, Samuel Shaw had an experience with a large vessel which effectively discouraged
the Americans from attempting to carry on their commerce
along the lines followed by the East India Company.

While in Canton on his second voyage, he ordered a ship
to be built in Quincy, Massachusetts, on the model of an
East-Indiaman. It was to be the largest vessel ever
launched from an American shipyard, eight hundred tons
burden, with length of keel one hundred and sixteen feet,
breadth of beam thirty-six feet, and depth of hold thirteen
feet. Specifications called for 'three Decks, and a round
house with a Stern Gallery from the round house, and
quarter gallery above and below, with thirty-two ports on

her Second Deck, and a forecastle on her Upper Deck.' 'It is the expectation of Messrs. Shaw & Randall,' read the contract for its construction, 'that they can produce from America such a ship as will bear the Inspection of the Most Critical Eye, both as to construction and workmanship.'

It was duly built, and in September, 1789, launched amid great excitement. People from Boston and all over the countryside flocked to Quincy to see it slide from the ways. The river and harbor were thick with boats of entranced spectators, the surrounding hills covered with loyal sons of Massachusetts, who found in this vessel, to which the name of their State was given, a proof and a promise of what Massachusetts shipbuilders could do.

A few months later, March 28, 1790, the *Massachusetts* sailed under the command of Captain Job Prince. After a stop at Batavia, where Shaw unsuccessfully attempted to dispose of part of her cargo, she reached China on September 30. The sensation the vessel created there fully lived up to all the builders' hopes. 'It surpassed even our most sanguine expectations that she meet the approbation of all the Europeans at Canton,' Captain Prince wrote to her designer, William Hackett, 'and tho there eyes were open to spy defects and there tounges ready to find fault, they confessed they could not.' It was universally admitted that the *Massachusetts* was 'as perfect a model as the state of the art would then permit.'

But these tributes to his vessel did not help Shaw to dispose of her cargo. The rebuff at Batavia had first disappointed his expectations and it was found at Canton that his large assortment of goods was unsalable. When he received an offer from the Danish East India Company to purchase the ship for sixty-five thousand dollars, a profit of some fifteen thousand dollars over its original cost, he accepted it with alacrity. The *Massachusetts* had proved to be a triumph of shipbuilding, but impracticable for American trade because the possible loss on a single cargo was too heavy a drain on its owners. Smaller vessels and smaller cargoes were more suited to the needs of the young commerce.

If the small size of most of the American vessels excited comment at Canton, no less wonder was caused by the youthfulness of their crews. They were largely of good American stock, with an admixture of English, Dutch, and Swedes, for it was a time when the youth of the Atlantic seaboard, and especially of New England, turned inevitably to the sea. At an age when to-day they would be in high school, they were at the close of the eighteenth century sailing before the mast; when to-day they might be in college, they were then in command of their ships; when to-day they might be entering business, they were then ship-owners and preparing to retire from the sea as established merchants.

There was, for example, the voyage of the eighty-nine-ton Boston sloop *Union*, which Samuel Eliot Morison has called 'the most remarkable youthful exploit in this bright dawn of Pacific adventure.' The captain of this little vessel, which in 1794 was the first sloop-rigged vessel to circle the globe, was John Boit, Jr. He had already been to Canton and the Northwest Coast as fifth mate of the *Columbia*, yet on this second voyage he was only nineteen years old. The comment of the Boston 'Centinel' on the end of his successful expedition was merely the brief notice among arrivals in port: 'Sloop *Union*, Boit, Canton.'

Another voyage about the same time was that of the Salem ship *Benjamin*, commanded by Captain Nathaniel Silsbee, later United States Senator. He had already followed the sea for five years and like Boit had reached the hoary age of nineteen. His mate was but a year older and only one member of the crew was over twenty-one. This was the second mate, a veteran of twenty-four, and he had to be discharged at Mauritius for insubordination. The voyage of these youngsters was so successful that it returned to the owners four or five times their capital investment.

Richard Cleveland, then eighteen, was Captain Silsbee's clerk on the *Benjamin* and it was only six years later that he was sailing his little cutters to the Northwest Coast and about the Indian Ocean. Silsbee's two brothers had their own commands like Captain Nathaniel before they were twenty. Five brothers in the Crowninshield family of Salem were all captains before they were twenty-one.

At a somewhat later period William Sturgis, who was virtually to control the trade between Canton and the Northwest Coast, went to sea at fourteen, was a captain at nineteen, and at twenty-eight formed the firm of Bryant and Sturgis. Robert B. Forbes, one of the best-known China merchants, was a third mate at sixteen, a captain at twenty, a shipowner at twenty-six, and a merchant at twenty-eight.

Matching the youth of these boys, who sailed the China coast so debonairly before they had attained their majority, was the inexperience in sailing Eastern waters and the ignorance of Eastern ports which they shared with older mariners. No one knows where the Americans got their first charts of the Pacific and in many cases navigation was apparently based on nothing more than crude maps. The *Grand Turk* was equipped with 'a few erroneous maps and charts, a sextant and a Guthrie's Grammar.' The *Benjamin* had neither charts nor chronometer and sailed by dead reckoning. The *Alliance*, the famous frigate once commanded by John Paul Jones and dispatched to Canton by Robert Morris, took an entirely unknown route south of Australia and did not drop anchor until it reached China. But early reports declared that it had no charts, 'for there were none to be had, but have Guthrie's Grammar.'

What was this mystic key to Oriental traffic mentioned, among many other voyages, in the case of the *Grand Turk* and the *Alliance*? 'Guthrie's Grammar, called a New System of Modern Geography,' was first issued in this country in 1795, so that it must have been on earlier English editions the first American travelers were forced to rely. Yet, even in 1807, when it was issued with a 'correct set of maps, engraved in a very superior manner,' all it contained were large-scale charts similar to, but not as accurate as, those found to-day in any geography book. The information they conveyed was supplemented by the thoughtful statement that 'it was in Asia, according to the sacred records that the all-wise Creator planted the Garden of Eden, in which he formed the first man and first woman, from whom the race of mankind was to spring.' The harassed mariner threading his way through Sunda Straits or beating up along the China coast might find this comforting to his religion, but hardly helpful to navigation.

Even if these vessels knew where they were going, however, so few and imperfect were the nautical instruments which they carried that they must often have reached their destinations by pure chance. For the *Benjamin* not to have a chronometer was the rule rather than the exception in the first days of the China trade. Yet Ebenezer Townsend, Jr., declared in 1797 that lunar observations, the only method of getting longitude without a chronometer, were just gaining popularity and few were the officers who knew how to make them. The *Massachusetts*, not only the largest but the best-equipped vessel of its day, had missed Java Head and lost three weeks on its voyage in 1790 'on account of our not having any chronometer on board, nor any officer who knew anything about lunar observations.' With Nathaniel Bowditch and the publication in 1801 of the 'Practical Navigator,' all this was to be changed, but in the eighties and nineties the Canton trade was carried on without benefit of accurate charts or accurate instruments.

If the dangers of uncharted coasts and unknown reefs and shoals were somehow miraculously avoided, there was still another risk the American ships had to face in running the gauntlet of pirate craft which hovered about the southern straits and along the China shore. Fleets of swift Malay proas lay in wait for the unwary and the price of safety was constant vigilance. Should a vessel become becalmed or run upon a reef in Sunda Straits, the native craft were apt to appear suddenly from nowhere ready to board the stricken boat, plunder its cargo and massacre its crew. When American ships were later to explore the South Seas this was to happen in the Fiji Islands again and again, but against the Malays and the pirates of the China coast, who at one time could muster a fleet of hundreds of vessels, the Americans usually succeeded in defending themselves.

In 1798, the *Betsy*, despite rigging and painted guns which gave it the appearance of a ship of war, was attacked by a fleet of twenty-nine proas. It had left Canton in company with a Philadelphia vessel, but on the first sign of danger this fair-weather friend had deserted the slower-sailing *Betsy* and Captain Fanning was left in a dying wind to defend himself as best he could. His ten real guns, eight four-pounders and two long six-pounders, were loaded with round shot and bags of musket balls, and the crew was

ordered to wait with lighted matches for the Malays'
approach. With hideous yelling they swept down upon the
little vessel until they were within musket shot. 'At this
moment,' wrote Captain Fanning, 'I clapped the helm a
weather, hauled up the courses, and the ship, quickly wearing off, brought her broadside as handsomely as mortal
could wish to bear directly on the proas.' The triumphant
attack was abruptly halted. A second broadside and the
fleet beat a frantic retreat with many of the proas well
riddled with shot and one completely disabled.

This action was off Sumatra. A few years later Captain
William Sturgis in the *Atahualpa*, loaded with three hundred thousand dollars in silver specie, beat off the attack of
sixteen Ladrone pirates in Macao roads. In his account of
the incident he tells of how he lit a cigar and swore he'd
throw it into a powder barrel rather than yield his ship.
One of his passengers, 'yellow as a sunflower' from an attack of jaundice, was completely cured by the excitement.

These two vessels were not the only ones prepared to
protect themselves from pirates. Every vessel of that day
carried heavy armaments. Shaw speaks of storing ten of the
guns of the *Empress of China* below decks while at Cape
Verde; the *Massachusetts*, pierced for thirty-six guns, carried
twenty six-pounders; the *Grand Turk* mounted twenty-two
guns; the sloop *Union* had ten carriage guns; and even the
*Experiment* carried six cannon. In addition to this artillery,
all ships carried musketry and full equipment of pikes and
cutlasses. So many of the captains and crews had sailed on
privateersmen that the profession of arms was no stranger
to them. They were ready and eager to beat off any attack
which threatened.

The route followed by vessels in the early trade was at
first directly to Canton, with perhaps brief stops at the

THE ASPASIA ROUNDING CAPE HORN

THE BETSY RETURNING INTO PORT

Cape Verde Islands or the Cape of Good Hope to take on fresh provisions, but more circuitous voyages were soon made. The *General Washington*, Captain Johnathan Donnison, a three-hundred-and-sixty-ton Providence vessel, as early as 1787 called at Madeira, Madras, and Pondicherry on its way to Canton and on the return voyage stopped at St. Helena, Ascension, and St. Eustatius. The *Hope* in the second year of the trade set a fashion generally followed thereafter of calling at Batavia. Calcutta and Bombay were often stations on the way to China and freighting Indian cotton to Canton became a profitable branch of Eastern commerce. Mauritius and Reunion, then known as Ile de France and Ile de Bourbon, were regular ports of call.

Nor was the direct route home any more common after the first few voyages. Calls were made at European ports from Genoa to St. Petersburg. Canton's teas might be sold at Hamburg or at Leghorn, its silks in Spain, or its nankeens in France. We find Samuel Shaw, who made his way to Bombay and Calcutta after his second voyage, making plans in 1791 to take his Canton merchandise to the former port, 'thence freight it to Ostend, and, accompanying it myself, to dispose of it there, and arrive in America in time to sail the ensuing season for China.' Tea was shipped to Hamburg by the Americans in 1796 according to the reports of the East India Company, and the next year to Holland and Spain. These newcomers to world trade were everywhere. Few were the ports, either of Europe or Asia, which did not have the opportunity to marvel at the efficiency with which such small vessels, manned by such young crews, carried on their thriving trade.

As for the cargoes taken to and from Canton, they may best be learned from the manifests or receipt books of those ships whose papers have been preserved among their owners' files or in the sea chests of their captains and super-cargoes. For the *Empress of China*, for the *Experiment*, for the *Grand Turk*, and for the *Astrea*, a Salem vessel sent out in 1789 by Elias Hasket Derby, we have records which give an intimate picture of the Canton trade before the opening of the nineteenth century.

The clerk of the *Empress of China* was Frederick Moli-neux and it is from his little cloth-covered book marked 'Receits' and dated 'Canton in China, October 8th, 1784,' that a fascinating account can be gleaned of Captain John Green's personal transactions while in the Chinese port.

'Rece'd at Canton October 9th, of F. Molineux for accot. of Capt. Green ten Dollars being in part of a contract for several Ombrellas' is the first item in this book, signed by 'Way-fang — Ombrella maker the upper part of Hog Lane'; and it is in this form that all Captain Green's pur-chases from the Canton merchants are carefully recorded. They included boxes of lacquered ware, 'six hundred La-dies Silk Mitts' at a cost of $100, a box of 'Chow Chow Articles' purchased from 'Tyane, Image Maker,' for $38, several invoices of silk, tea, nankeens, and chinaware, some 'cassia and flowers,' 'two tubbs or China Bowls and One Dish,' thirty dollars' worth of fans, 'six pr. sattin shoes Ladies,' and, most carefully receipted of all, exactly one hundred and thirteen pairs of 'Sattin Breeches at 1½ Dollars p' pair' which were purchased from 'Apan, Taylor on the lower Bridge.'

Captain Green also bought certain sundries for the ac-count of both Robert Morris and Mrs. Morris. We read that on December 2, 1784, there was paid to 'Eshing, Paper Mercht.' the sum of 'One Hundred Dollars for Paper Hangings for Robt. Morris Esq. the Borders not being included,' and a few days later forty-nine dollars was receipted by 'Howqua Lacquer Man' as payment for 'a dressing Boxe & four Lacquered Fans for Mrs. Morris.' Two bundles of 'Bamboo silk Mounted Window blinds' were also purchased for the wife of the principal owner of the *Empress of China.*

Only one receipt in this book refers to Samuel Shaw, and that bears his own signature acknowledging payment of forty-two dollars, 'being in full the amot. Sales of two Barrells Tarr to the ship Le Necker, Capt. Woolmore.'

In the writing of a different clerk there are also receipts for certain purchases of Captain Green made on the second voyage of the *Empress of China* in 1786. Here are one hundred pairs of satin breeches, satin shoes of different colors, a blue coat and satin breeches, certain pictures painted on glass, a 'Table sett Nankin Blue and White China 170 pieces mark'd I W N. 1,' six jars of sweetmeats, lacquer ware, '24 Mother pearl mounted fanns & two feather brushes,' paper and silk fans, 'Pegodas & 4 Chinese images,' and 'six paint Boxes & paints in Watter Collours.' Finally, one of the last items, in which Captain Green himself signed a receipt for five dollars, records the purchase of 'a tea Sett China, for Mrs. Wilkinson, a sett Mother Pearl Counters for Mrs. Bunner & 6 tooth brushes for myself.'

The papers of Captain Dean of the *Experiment* — faded statements of his accounts made out for the owners with receipts for everything he bought in Canton — tell the whole story of the preparations made for the venturesome voyage of this little eighty-ton sloop in the wake of the *Empress of China.* It was made possible by the subscriptions of a group of eighteen New York merchants who bought nineteen shares of stock in the enterprise at £600 each. The cost of the *Experiment* and its equipment was

£2570/10; that of its cargo, £8860. For several weeks the subscribers met every Tuesday at six at the Coffee House to work out their plans, and the final agreement was drawn up on November 17, 1785.

The most important item in the vessel's cargo was eighteen boxes of silver dollars. Fifty boxes and fifteen casks of ginseng were also loaded, a considerable quantity of furs including squirrel, fox, one bearskin, and 'three wild catts,' and several small shipments of tar, turpentine, tobacco, snuff, and Madeira. As for the stores with which a vessel of this period was equipped, Captain Dean's papers afford some interesting details. Among receipts for sailmakers' and coopers' charges, bills for wharfage and anchors, are the receipts for the *Experiment's* guns and gun carriages, for supplies of pork, beef, cider, bread, Russian duck, gunpowder, candles, Madeira, brandy, butter, wine, medicine, and mathematical instruments. There was a special bill of £2/7 for physic; the mathematical instruments cost £5/9/4, and for charts and directions from John Thompson and Abraham Evening there was paid the excessive sum of 16s. 6d.

Wages of the crew — master, two mates, five seamen, and two boys — were estimated over the period from November 1, 1785, to April 25, 1787. Captain Dean received £199/13/5; his black cabin boy, Prince, £34/1/4. The owners' letter of instructions was couched in general terms. Captain Dean was to receive a five per cent commission on all transactions at Canton, was warned to watch out for Javanese pirates, and otherwise told to use his own judgment.

At Canton the cargo of £8860 was sold for £19,000, and after payment of port charges and expenses ashore, the remainder was invested in Chinese goods. Some three hundred and eight chests of Hyson, a hundred chests of Souchong, eighty bales of nankeens, and thirty-one chests of chinaware were brought to New York and there sold for £37,000. Heavy expenses at home and customs duties cut down this profit but at that the voyage netted £9294/16, a return of better than seventy-two per cent on the original investment when the books were finally closed.

The *Grand Turk*, which sailed from Salem about the same time as the *Experiment* was leaving New York, was originally intended for Mauritius and proceeded to Canton only because the market at the French island was unusually depressed. Its cargo was consequently more general. The complete invoice shows:

10 bbls. of pitch, 10 bbls. of tar, 75 bbls. superfine flour, 6 tierces of rice, 35 hogsheads tobacco, 49 furkins New York butter, 20 Casks Claret Wine, 483 Bars Iron, 12 Hogsheads Loaf Sugar, 50 cases of oil, 20 Boxes Chocolate, 22 Boxes Prunes, 20 Crates Earthenware, 26 Casks Brandy, 163½ bbls. of Beef, 9 Casks Ginseng, 30 Puncheons Granada Rum, 42 Casks Coniac Brandy, 7 Casks Bacon and Hams, 7 Boxes English Mold Candles, 50 Boxes Spermacety Candles, 100 Boxes Mould Candles, 27 Boxes Tallow Candles, 32 Boxes Soap, 478 Furkins Butter, 579 Boxes Cheese, 123½ Bbls. Pork, 38 Kegs of Beef, 25 Baskets Aniseed, 14 Hogshads New Eng. Rum high proof, 20½ Hogshds Fish, 42 Bbls. of Beer, 4 Tierces of Bottled Beer, 4 Tierces of Porter, 9 Kegs of Pork.

This cargo totaled £7183/5/7. Stores, wages, and outfit were put at £2000 and an item of 'light cash' brought the total investment up to £9200.

After calling at Mauritius, where it disposed of some of this cargo and took on as freight for Canton some shipments of ebony wood, ginseng, gold thread, cloth, and betel nuts, the *Grand Turk* reached China in September. By the end of the year it had exchanged its varied New England products and sailed for home with a cargo of Chinese goods valued at £23,218. The return manifest shows:

240 Chests Bohea Tea, 175 ½ Chests Bohea Tea, 2 Chests Hyson Tea, 52 Chests Souchong, 32 Chests Bohea Congo, 130 Chests Cassia, 10 Chests Cassia Bud, 75 Boxes China, quantity hides from Cape, 10 Casks Wine, 1 Box paper.

Four years later, in 1789, another of Elias Hasket Derby's ships, the *Astrea*, sailed for Canton under Captain James Magee, who had formerly commanded the *Hope*, with one of Boston's future merchants, Thomas Handasyd Perkins, as its supercargo. It had become Derby's custom to spend from six months to a year in assembling the cargo for an Eastern voyage. Iron, duck, and hemp were brought from the Baltic; wine and lead from France, Spain, and Madeira; rum from the West Indies; and flour, tobacco, and ship provisions from New York, Philadelphia, and Richmond. Furthermore, his own shipments were supplemented by those private adventures which were a part of New England's commercial traditions. The captain and supercargo were allowed a certain amount of free space in the vessel, while other friends and business associates of the owners could, upon payment of freight charges and commissions, place small shipments in the hands of the supercargo and empower him to trade for them at Canton on the best terms he could obtain. This system not only made it easier to raise the capital for such long voyages, but it created as nothing else could an interest in the products of the Far East. None was so poor but he could make some small speculation in the China trade. If he could not send out a bag of silver dollars which might net him several chests of tea at a tidy profit, at least he could entrust to a willing supercargo a few boxes of spermaceti candles or some barrels of salmon which would bring him a fine piece of silk or a set of china dishes.

Consequently we find that the *Astrea* carried a cargo fully as miscellaneous as that of the *Grand Turk*, part of it on the owner's account and part on that of private adventurers. It was an undertaking in which almost all of Salem seems to have participated. There was a quantity of ginseng in the cargo, many ventures of bags of silver dollars on nine per cent commission, a great deal of wine and beer, fifty barrels of salmon, a hundred tons of iron, fifty barrels of tar, fifty boxes of chocolate, five hundred and ninety-eight firkins of butter, three hundred and forty-five boxes of spermaceti candles, a hundred and fifteen tubs of steel, forty-eight barrels of beef, and three hundred and thirty-six barrels of flour.

Magee and Perkins had in their own name one pipe of Madeira wine and one pipe of port, two hundred and fifty pounds of loaf sugar, four cases of Geneva, twenty gallons of brandy, ninety-five dozen bottles of rappee snuff, and five hundred and fifty-two pounds of manufactured tobacco. One adventurer sent out two boxes of women's shoes; another nineteen dozen handkerchiefs. Folger Pope tried his luck with a phaëton and harness complete, while James Bott sent a box of saddlery.

Derby's instructions to his captain and supercargo were that the *Astrea* was first to stop at Batavia and there endeavor to pick up sugar, coffee, saltpeter, nutmeg, and pepper — the sugar to be used as a floor for the tea they were to purchase at Canton and the pepper to be stowed in the far peak where it would not injure the tea. For himself he wanted some ginger and fifteen or twenty pounds in curiosities, whatever china cups or saucers might be bought to be put in the crop of the bilge.

The season in which the *Astrea* reached Canton found the greatest number of American vessels in port that had ever been in China. Derby himself had four ships there of his own and the market was so glutted with New England products that his representatives were forced to sell two of them to be able to buy sufficient cargo to lade the other two. The goods sent out by the *Astrea* sold for twenty thousand dollars less than their original cost. Nevertheless, it loaded sufficient teas, silks, chinaware, and nankeens to have to pay duty at Salem of $27,109.18.

The return manifest shows that Magee and Perkins on their joint account imported 65 chests of Hyson, 35 chests of Bohea, 10 one-half chests of Bohea, 3 boxes of chinaware, 15 cases of nankeens, and 1 case of silk. Also in Magee's name were 10 boxes of merchandise, 6 bundles of window-frames, 2 bundles of floor mats, 7 boxes of images, 6 boxes of pictures, 2 lacquerware tea boxes, 4 small boxes, 2 small bundles of hair, 1 small box of sundries, 2 ivory boxes, paper hangings, 4 tubs of sugar candy, 1 box of ribbons, and 'one bagg farmerie.' When we read such a list it is easy to understand why the fine mansions of Salem's merchants became veritable museums of the curios of the Far East. Few were the housewives who could resist the chance to get a lacquer tea-set, some Chinese scrolls, or at least a dozen china dishes after the return of one of Derby's ships from the long eastward voyage.

Sometimes, as we find in later records, some Salem maid or matron, jealous of her neighbor's Oriental finery, might give such a minute commission as this one, signed by Henrietta Elkins, for the captain of the ship *Messenger*: 'Please to purchase if at Calcutta two net bead with draperies; if at Batavia or any spice market, nutmegs, and mace, or if at Canton, Two Canton Crape shawls of the enclosed colors at

$5 per shawl. Enclosed is $10.' And in the papers of the
same ship is an order from Mrs. Mary Townsend for 'one
Tureen 14 by 10 inches, China.' It is somewhat difficult to
imagine the officers of one of our modern freighters accepting such shopping commissions from the ladies of their
community!

One more quotation may give a still further idea of the
miscellany of Oriental goods sometimes imported for the
benefit of New England households. When the *Rising Sun*
returned from Canton in 1793 to its home port of Providence, an advertisement in the Providence 'Gazette'
announced as freshly arrived from China:

Fresh Bohea tea of the first quality, in Chests, Half, and Quarter
Chests, China, a great Variety, Sattins, Lutestrings, Persians,
Taffetas, of different Qualities, black and other Colours, A Variety
of fashionable Silks and Silk and Cotton, for Gentlemen's Summer
Wear, Nankeens, Elegant Sattin Shoe-Patterns, Pearl Buttons
with Gold Figures, Superfine Lambskins, Ivory and lacquered
Ware, Tea-Caddies, A large Assortment of lacquered Tea-Trays,
Waiters, Bottle-stands, &c. &c. Silk Handkerchiefs, Hair Rib-
bons, Cinnamons and Cinnamon Buds, Black Pepper, 200 Boxes
excellent Sugar, &c.

So it was that under these conditions of trade and with
these cargoes America's commerce with the Far East had
quickly assumed an importance which more than justified
the optimistic reports which Samuel Shaw had made upon
the return of the *Empress of China* from its first voyage. He
himself was not destined to see its full development. He
died homeward bound on the ship *Washington* in 1794 at the
very time when the China trade was winning recognition as
an expansive outlet for the energies of maritime America.
But if his country did not have the opportunity to reward
his services in any direct way, it at least paid him the

tribute of doing everything possible to further and protect
the trade which he had inaugurated. Special duties were
laid upon goods from the Far East not imported directly
from the place of manufacture in American ships, discounts
were given for the importation of tea, and we find Alexander
Hamilton urging at the third session of the First Congress
that the privileges of those trading in tea should be still
further extended. The importance of the China trade,
he declared, 'appears to lay claim to the patronage of the
Government.'

What was the effect of this new commercial activity? It
aroused the forebodings of the English for one thing. While
the Constitutional Convention was still sitting in Philadelphia, the British agents in America, Sir John Temple in
New York and Phineas Bond in Philadelphia, reported
nervously on the threat to English commerce in voyages
which were not only bringing tea to America, but also carrying it to European markets which the British considered
their special preserves. Bond thought it was not yet too late
to save the situation. 'If an early check or restraint can be
thrown in their way, either by thwarting their credit, or by
withholding the articles suitable for their commerce,' he
wrote to Lord Carmarthen, 'I am convinced they would
never rally.' And in a vain attempt to put this suggestion
into effect and 'perfectly unhinge this trade,' the representatives of the East India Company in Canton were instructed
'to use every endeavor to prevent the subjects of Great
Britain from assisting or encouraging in any shape the
American commerce.'

It was too late, however. The few voyages we have
sketched give a picture of a trade which British influence
could not hope to 'unhinge' so easily. In the United States
the lack of a national monetary system, the decentralization

of political authority, insufficient capital, and British competition had combined to hamper the recovery of domestic trade, but foreign commerce had risen above these difficulties. It was fast expanding and destined in the last decade of the eighteenth century to multiply fourfold. Thomas Jefferson had written that 'it might be better for us to abandon the ocean altogether, that being the element whereon we shall be principally exposed to jostle with other nations, to leave to others to bring what we shall want, and to carry what we can spare.' The merchants of the young republic knew better.

About 1790 it was estimated that the China trade accounted for approximately one seventh of the country's imports. It was one branch of our commerce in which English competition offered no effective threat to American activities. It brought the greatest profits of any branch of our foreign trade, founded the fortunes of a long line of merchants in New York, Philadelphia, Boston, and Salem, and attracted the best ships and most daring seamen of the Atlantic ports.

# CHAPTER IV

## THE NORTHWEST COAST

Toward the end of the eighteenth century it became evident that ginseng and the other miscellaneous products which the Americans were carrying to Canton had but a limited market, while too great a reliance upon specie constituted a heavy drain on the slender resources of the United States. Something else had to be found which the American merchants could sell to the Chinese in sufficient quantity to lade their vessels with the tea and silks for which the demand at home was so pressing. Consequently the history of the China trade for the next two decades is that of an indefatigable search for articles of trade which would meet the exacting tastes of the merchants and mandarins of the Chinese port.

One such product was found in the rich furs of the sea otter which could be bought from the Indians of the Northwest Coast of America for a few trinkets. When it became generally known that these pelts fetched high prices in Canton, American vessels were every year skirting the rugged coast-line of what is now Oregon, Washington, and British Columbia and carrying on vigorous barter with its savage and often treacherous Indian tribes. It was a trade which for a time was the most important branch of the commerce with China, and one of its ultimate results was greatly to strengthen American claims to the territory now constituting our Northwest States through the discovery of the Columbia River and the settlement at Astoria.

The chance discovery that sea-otter furs were so valuable in the eyes of the Chinese was made at the time of the voyages of the English explorer, Captain James Cook. On his last expedition along the uncharted shores of America, a number of his seamen bartered with the Indians for some of the glossy black skins for their own use. A great many of these furs were lost or spoiled on the voyage across the Pacific, but when the ships reached Canton, the English sailors were amazed at the fabulous prices which the Chinese merchants offered them for whatever skins they had left. They quickly sold all they had for a total of ten thousand dollars and then almost mutinied in a vain attempt to force their officers to return to the Northwest Coast and take on a full cargo.

One of these seamen was American born, a corporal of marines named John Ledyard, whose adventurous life has been recorded by Jared Sparks. After the conclusion of the voyage, Ledyard deserted from the British Navy and returned to his own country, there to publish in 1783 a journal of his travels. In it he tells of the great wealth of furs to be found in the Northwest and of the excitement of his fellow seamen when they found in Canton that 'skins which did not cost the purchaser sixpence sterling, sold in China for 100 dollars.'

Never was there a more vigorous promoter of a new trade than this John Ledyard. In New York, Boston, Paris, and London he tried to urge hesitant and skeptical merchants to undertake an experimental voyage between the Northwest Coast and Canton, but persistent ill-luck followed every move he made. In this country his scheme was called wild and visionary, although at least once he was within an ace of success. Robert Morris was persuaded of the practicality of his idea and went so far as to commission Ledyard to find a ship to undertake the voyage. Then at the last moment the plans were changed and the vessel Ledyard had obtained, in all probability the *Empress of China*, was dispatched directly to Canton with a cargo of ginseng instead of attempting the passage about Cape Horn and up the American coast.

After this disappointment, Ledyard went to Paris, where he talked with Thomas Jefferson, who seems to have approved of his plans despite his aversion to foreign commerce. Then he reached an agreement with John Paul Jones for a Northwest voyage, only to have it too fall through, like the project planned with Robert Morris. Ledyard sorrowfully went on to London. Here he actually started on a voyage for his El Dorado, with the idea of returning overland to Virginia, but his ship was recalled.

We next find him setting out, upon Jefferson's advice, on a land journey across Siberia with the intention of making his way to Kamchatka, across the Bering Sea, and then down the American coast to Nootka Sound. He got as far east as Yakutsk, but was then arrested, supposedly on orders instigated by the jealousy of the Russian-American Fur Company, and, after being held a prisoner for some time, he was escorted back to the European border. For all his persistence, his enthusiasm, and his daring, Ledyard was not to see the beginning of the trade he had fought for so energetically. He gave up hope of persuading the world to believe in him and, having turned his zeal for exploration into new channels, he died at Cairo in 1788.

The seed he had helped to sow was bound to grow. No sooner had he deserted the Northwest for Egypt than both English and French vessels began to find their way to the coast, and in Boston a group of six merchants — Joseph Barrell, Charles Bulfinch, Samuel Brown, John Derby, Crowell Hatch, and John Marden Pintard — were planning to follow the advice which just a few years before they had so casually scorned. The publication of Cook's journals and the reports brought home by Shaw had at last convinced them that Ledyard had known what he was talking about when he had so enthusiastically sung the praises of his precious coast.

Having raised fifty thousand dollars capital, these six Boston merchants prepared to send to the Northwest two vessels, the *Columbia*, two hundred and twelve tons, Captain John Kendrick, and the *Lady Washington*, a sloop of ninety tons, Captain Robert Gray. Both officers had served on privateersmen and both ships were heavily armed. A cargo of iron tools and such trinkets as buttons, beads, jews'-harps, earrings, and snuffboxes was obtained, special sea letters secured from Congress, and a medal struck off to commemorate the occasion. On September 30, 1787, the two vessels started upon a voyage which in the course of time was to lead to the establishment of an American empire in the Northwest far beyond the dreams of the statesmen who that very year were passing the Northwest Ordinance.

Making their way about Cape Horn, the first American vessels ever to attempt this dangerous passage, the *Columbia* and the *Lady Washington* ran into one of the fierce storms for which this part of the world is famous. Fighting their way amid drifting ice and blinding snow, the two ships became separated and did not meet again until eleven months after they had left Boston, when first the *Lady Washington* and then the *Columbia* crept into Nootka Sound. The little sloop under Captain Gray had already lost one man through Indian treachery when a shore party was ambushed at a cove, which they thereupon named Murderers' Harbor. The *Columbia* had escaped savage attack, but its crew were so stricken with scurvy by the time it reached the coast that the seamen of the *Lady*

*Washington* had to come to their aid before they could take down sail and anchor the ship.

After such misadventures it was too late to attempt any trade that season. These pioneers of the Northwest set up a camp on shore at Friendly Cove and put their armorers to work making their scrap iron into 'chisels' — rough tools about eight inches long — which among the Indians passed for currency. With the coming of spring they began to barter for furs. A prime sea-otter skin was found to be worth from six to eight of these pieces of iron, a blanket, or a looking-glass; six furs were the trading equivalent for a musket. At one harbor, where the Indians flocked off to trade in a veritable fleet of canoes, two hundred skins were obtained for two hundred chisels, and this rich haul proved in Canton to be worth more than six thousand dollars.

In July, 1789, Captain Gray, who had now assumed command of the expedition, although Kendrick had been its first leader, changed to the *Columbia*, and leaving the *Lady Washington* on the coast sailed for Canton. In the Chinese port the firm which had been established by Shaw and Randall disposed of his cargo of furs and the *Columbia* was loaded with some three hundred and fifty chests of Bohea tea. Sailing again in February, it kept on its westward course and on August 10, 1790, proudly entered Boston Harbor. It had logged more than fifty thousand miles and carried the American flag around the world for the first time.

The *Columbia's* cargo failed to realize the profits its owners had expected, but its voyage had proved that the fur trade held out tremendous possibilities. The vessel was no sooner in port than preparations were commenced for a second voyage, and before the year was over, it had set out again for the coast on the expedition which discovered

the great river of the Northwest to which the *Columbia* lent
its name.

Furthermore, the *Columbia's* first venture inspired other
Boston merchants to follow its lead, and in the same year
in which it returned to the Coast, four other vessels were
on its trail. Another decade and in 1801 fifteen American
ships carried to Canton eighteen thousand skins worth
more than half a million dollars. Boston had initiated the
trade; Boston kept a virtual monopoly of it. Rivals from
both England and other American ports found it hard to
compete successfully. From 1790 to 1818 there were one
hundred and eight American vessels on the Coast as compared with twenty-two from England, and in a list in which
the names of sixty-three of these ships are given, fifty-three
prove to be from Boston. To the Indians who knew the
English as 'King George men,' the Americans were known
as 'Boston men.'

It was a venturesome, exciting, and profitable trade, this
three-cornered commerce in which iron chisels were exchanged for the furs of the sea otter and they in turn traded
at Canton for teas and silks. Rounding Cape Horn was a
first challenge to the seamanship and courage of the crews
of vessels which averaged from one hundred to two hundred
and fifty tons, but the wild and rugged coastline of Northwest America presented even greater hazards. 'Its mountains, rising in magnificent amphitheatres, covered with
evergreen forests, with here and there a verdant plain near
the shore, and a snow-capt mountain in the background,'
may have offered, as one captain rhapsodized in his sea
journal, 'a view grand and sublime in the highest degree,'
but there was another side to the picture. It was to be found
in the 'sunken rocks, strong tides, fogs, calms, no bottom
for anchoring, and a large proportion of bad weather' which

was just as typical of the austere shore-line which stretches from Alaska to the mouth of the Columbia.

It was the custom of the Nor'westmen to spend one or two seasons on the coast, putting into any cove or inlet where they might find an Indian village or slowly drifting along the shore in the hope that the Indians would find them and come out to the vessel in fur-laden canoes. Prices for the otter pelts naturally went up as more and more ships came out and soon it was a shrewd trader who could always be sure of his profits.

There were certain staples in the trade — cutlery, iron-ware, tin, chisels, knives, nails, clothing, blankets, beads, molasses, sugar, muskets, and rum — but fashions changed. Sometimes the Indians scorned blue cloth and would buy only red, or insisted upon greatcoats or muskets at a rate of exchange which made trade impossible. Again, the very next village might be almost willing to give its furs away. On one occasion green glass beads were in such demand that they sold two for a skin, while another time the members of an iron-impoverished tribe enthusiastically hailed the approach of an American vessel and 'instantly stripped themselves, and for a moderate quantity of large spike nails, we received sixty fine skins.'

On the voyage of the *Hope*, Joseph Ingraham, who in 1790 had been home only five weeks from the *Columbia's* first voyage before setting out again, found that the Indians on his first stop at the Queen Charlotte Islands, off the coast of what is now British Columbia, were all wearing jackets and trousers. Consequently they had no use for his cloth until he had the brilliant idea of sewing bright brass buttons on it. Nor did inspiration stop here. He set his armorer to work making iron collars and established a vogue so popular that it profited him to the extent of three skins, worth about forty dollars each at Canton, for each of these clumsy necklaces which his forge could turn out.

Thanks to this ingenuity and to the thoroughness with which he bargained for every skin in every village he visited, Ingraham collected eight hundred and fifty skins in his first month and in another three weeks had a full cargo of fourteen hundred. Prices unfortunately were low at the time he reached Canton, but he sold his furs for thirty thousand dollars. This sum he invested in tea, which was freighted back to America, while he returned to the coast to make another haul.

The fad he had introduced had changed before he arrived. His rivals had copied his popular style of iron collars and overdone it. Too many ships were on the coast, trade was slow, and in three months' cruising about the shores of Vancouver Island he could obtain only five hundred and fifty skins.

In 1802, William Sturgis, a sea captain who wrote that a prime sea-otter fur was the most beautiful natural object he had ever seen 'excepting a beautiful woman and a lovely infant,' collected no less than six thousand skins. But he had also noticed, with an eye for still greater profits, that the Indians were using ermine pelts for currency. On his return to Boston, he promptly sent to the Leipsic Fair and bought five thousand of these skins which were included in the cargo for his next voyage to the coast. He found the Indians glad to exchange a sea-otter skin, worth that year fifty dollars at Canton, for five of his ermine pelts, the latter having cost Captain Sturgis exactly thirty cents apiece!

Trade under these conditions did not make for stability. Sometimes a voyage would prove to be a losing venture; another time an investment of a few thousand dollars might mean furs worth a hundred thousand in China. The cargo

of the *Columbia* on her second voyage netted $90,000 at
Canton. Captain Sturgis once turned $50,000 into $284,000,
and Captain John Suter on a single voyage obtained enough
skins to invest $156,743.21 in Chinese tea which at home
sold for $261,343.18. But what made the Northwest trade
far more of a speculative undertaking than any fluctuation
in the price of furs were the risks which the American vessels ran from Indian treachery. There were many occasions
when the natives were not content to satisfy their lust for
iron collars or glass beads by peaceful barter.

On his first voyage Captain Gray had lost one man at
Murderers' Harbor; on his second, three of the crew were
killed in a surprise attack at Massacre Cove. Captain
Kendrick in the *Lady Washington* had a lucky escape from a
situation which might have taken an even greater toll of
life. The Indians, whom on one occasion he had too trust-
ingly allowed aboard his sloop, suddenly seized his arms
chest and, holding him captive on his own quarter deck,
drove the crew into the hold. But while the savages were
gayly proceeding to divide up the articles of trade which
the *Lady Washington* carried, Captain Kendrick laid his
plans. He shouted down to his men in the hold to muster
whatever weapons they could — which amounted to two
pistols, a musket, and two cutlasses — and to make a dash
for the deck when he should call out 'Follow me.' Soon the
Indian chief, who had been on the quarter deck, started
below. Kendrick immediately sprang on the savage and
shouted his command. His men rushed out and within
five minutes had won possession of the deck, broken open
the arms chest, and killed forty of the Indians without
losing a man.

These lessons were not lost upon the later traders. Every
ship was heavily armed — cannon, muskets, pistols, cut-

lasses, and pikes — and when trade was in progress boarding-nets would be tied up and only a few unarmed Indians allowed on shipboard at a time. Yet no precaution could entirely do away with the danger of attack. Should a vessel become becalmed or run on one of those sunken rocks with which the coast was studded, it lay almost at the mercy of the Indians, who could muster their long war canoes by the hundred.

Captain Cleveland was once becalmed in his little fifty-ton cutter and suddenly found his vessel surrounded by twenty-six native war canoes with some five hundred savages armed to the teeth with muskets, spears, and daggers. He had only two four-pounders and a pair of blunderbusses mounted on the stern to defend his ship against attack, but he immediately had his cannon loaded with bags of musket balls and served out two muskets and two pistols to each member of his crew. All day they lay helpless, standing by their guns with lighted matches, expecting each moment the onslaught they could not long hope to resist.

But the Indians hesitated and when that night they went ashore, Cleveland took quick advantage of a light breeze which sprang up toward morning and got his ship under way. It was just in time. They soon met a number of additional Indian canoes hurrying to the cove they had just left. It was doubtless because the attack had been delayed for the arrival of these reënforcements that the cutter had been able to escape.

A few days later and the vessel was again faced with the same danger under even more helpless conditions. It struck a sunken reef, and as the tide went out the cutter heeled over more and more until it was hanging on the rocks at an angle of forty-five degrees. Unable to stand on deck, the crew crowded into a sixteen-foot boat, where with muskets loaded they watched fearfully for the approach of any Indians.

'Our situation,' Cleveland wrote in the narrative of his voyages, 'was now one of the most painful anxiety, no less from the immediate prospect of losing our vessel, and the rich cargo we had collected with so much toil, than from apprehension of being discovered in this defenceless state by some of the hostile tribes by which we were surrounded.'

More than ten hours were spent in this 'agonizing state of suspense' when a sudden wind meant the loss of the vessel and sight of a canoe meant immediate attack, but at last the tide came in. No Indian canoes had appeared and Cleveland thankfully wrote that 'at half past twelve in the night we had the indescribable pleasure of seeing her afloat again.'

In 1805, Captain John D'Wolf in the *Juno*, two hundred and fifty tons, also ran on the rocks during the night. In his case morning brought not the tide but a fleet of canoes by which the stricken vessel was quickly surrounded. D'Wolf boldly told the Indians that he had merely put his vessel ashore to mend its copper sheathing and set his men to work calking the jagged holes which his misadventure had made in the bottom of his ship. He then cleverly enticed one of the Indian chiefs aboard the *Juno* and held him as a hostage against any treachery. When the tide at last came in, the ship was righted and with high water the chief was returned to his canoe and the *Juno* sailed off safely.[1]

Not always was escape so easy, however. In 1802, the *Boston*, Captain John Salter, which was cruising along the

---

[1] The damage done the *Juno* had one curious result. Captain D'Wolf decided to sell his ship at the Russian settlement at New Archangel (Sitka) and to set off for Europe overland. He was thus the first American to cross Siberia.

THE BOSTON TAKEN BY SAVAGES AT NOOTKA SOUND

coast with a cargo of English cloth, Dutch blankets, beads, looking-glasses, rum, and molasses, was suddenly attacked as it lay in Friendly Cove on Nootka Sound. The mistake had been made of allowing too many Indians on board ship, and when their chief, incensed by some fancied insult, gave his men the signal to attack, it found the crew of the *Boston* totally unprepared. Only two of the Americans survived, and one of them, John Jewitt, the ship's armorer, has left an exciting account of his 'adventures and sufferings.'

Working in the ship's hold, Jewitt heard a fierce struggle going on above him and ran up. 'Scarcely was my head above deck,' he wrote, 'when I was caught by the hair by one of the savages, and lifted from my feet; fortunately for me, my hair being short, and the ribbon with which it was tied slipping, I fell from his hold into the steerage. As I was falling, he struck at me with an axe, which cut a deep gash in my forehead, and penetrated the skull, but in consequence of his losing his hold, I luckily escaped the full force of the blow; which, otherwise, would have cleft my head in two. I fell stunned and senseless upon the floor.'

When he later regained consciousness and was hauled on deck, he was greeted by six naked savages covered with the blood of his murdered comrades and threatening his own life with upraised daggers. On the quarter deck in a grisly row lay the heads of Captain Salter and twenty-five of the crew. The intervention of the chief saved Jewitt's life. He was known to be the armorer and the Indians intended to put his skill at the forge to work for their own advantage. So he was carried off as a prisoner, and when later another survivor of the massacre was discovered hiding in the hold, Jewitt also managed to save him by representing the man as his father. Together the two men lived as slaves of their

captors for some three years until finally rescued by the
brig *Lydia*, Captain Hill.

In 1811, the New York ship *Tonquin* was sent out by
John Jacob Astor, under the command of Lieutenant J.
Thorn, of the United States Navy, with a crew of twenty-
one and thirty-three passengers, to establish what Astor
hoped would be a permanent colony on the Columbia
River. After various adventures, which included the loss of
eight men while making their way across the bar at the
Columbia's mouth, the settlement of Astoria was founded.
Leaving the colonists to open up their trade with the
Indians and to assemble a cargo of furs which another of
Astor's ships was expected to take to Canton, the *Tonquin*
then proceeded up the coast toward Nootka Sound.

On the way Captain Thorn, who seems to have been of an
irascible temper, quarreled with one of the native chiefs
while in the Straits of Juan de Fuca and drove him from his
ship. The next day trading continued as usual, and so confident was Thorn of the peacefulness of the Indians, despite
the incident of the day before, that all ordinary precautions
were omitted. The Indians were allowed on board in great
numbers and the ship's officers did not even wear their side-
arms. They were helpless when with blood-curdling war
cries the Indians at a given signal drew out knives and
bludgeons from beneath their bundles of furs and rushed
upon the crew.

Captain Thorn tried to defend himself with his pocket
knife, but was struck down. The rest of the crew struggled
as best they could, and after a fierce fight, in which many
of them lost their lives, the Indians were finally driven off.
An ominous calm then settled down over the ship. That
night there was no move either at escape or at a second
attack, but in the morning four sailors tried to get away

ATTACK AND MASSACRE OF CREW OF SHIP TONQUIN BY THE SAVAGES OF THE NORTHWEST COAST

in a small boat. Several Indian canoes started off in pursuit and the fate of the sailors was never known.

About the same time the savages again attacked the strangely still vessel and it was boarded by some five hundred wildly yelling Indians. Then suddenly there was a terrific explosion. The ship was totally destroyed, some two hundred Indians killed, and not a single member of the *Tonquin's* crew of twenty-one left to tell the tale. The only survivor of the tragedy, and the man from whom the fate of the vessel was finally learned by the settlers at Astoria, was the Indian interpreter. But he could not tell whether that final explosion was accidental or whether some wounded member of the crew took this final revenge upon the Indians by firing the ship's magazine.

Back at the mouth of the Columbia, Astor's colonists escaped Indian attack, but their venture came to a sad end. With the outbreak of the War of 1812, the settlers were fearful of capture by the British and, consulting their own interests rather than those of Astor, who had made every effort to keep them supplied despite the danger of seizure of his vessels by the British, they sold out the American company to its British rivals. Astoria as an American colony was no more and its founder's grandiose scheme to establish a great settlement on the Columbia River which might forever supply the furs for Canton, 'that great mart for peltries,' died stillborn.

But it was not only for Astoria that the War of 1812 proved to be such a disruptive influence. The fur trade as a whole never recovered from the effect of Britain's interference and many of the ships driven off the coast by English sloops-of-war never returned. Between 1790 and 1812 the average importation of sea-otter skins into Canton by the American traders was about twelve thousand each year; after the war this figure quickly dropped and the period from 1812 to 1834 showed average annual imports of about two thousand skins. Then the trade was practically over. Another decade and we find that statistics on sea-otter skins have disappeared.

The war, of course, was not wholly responsible for the end of the fur trade. If its prospects had been brighter, the American vessels would have hurried back to the coast as soon as hostilities were over, but such poor reports were made by those vessels which did return that we find Perkins and Company as early as 1815 abandoning a proposed Northwest voyage. The simple fact was that furs were becoming scarce and the Indians putting such a high price on those they still offered for sale that the trade was no longer profitable. It was so dependent upon cheap barter that the gradual increase in the prices demanded by the Indians destined it to a slow and lingering death which the events of 1812 had simply accelerated.

# CHAPTER V

## HAWAII AND SPANISH AMERICA

Two thousand miles off the Northwest Coast, in mid-Pacific, a group of islands rises majestically out of the sea. Their glistening beaches are lined with cocoanut palms and banana trees and thick tropical foliage grows far up their wooded mountain-sides. To the American seamen of the Nor'westmen no contrast to the dour and forbidding coast they had left could have been more striking or more pleasing. Here was a friendly haven where 'refreshment' could be obtained under conditions almost idyllic, and sailors stricken with scurvy or worn from an exacting trade with treacherous Indians could be soothed by the warm breezes of the south.

The *Columbia* had stopped at what were then known as the Sandwich Islands and anchored off the white shores of 'Owhyhee' on its first voyage. Thereafter almost every vessel on the coast followed its example *en route* to Canton, and many of them, unable in a single season to secure their full cargo of sea-otter furs, would spend the winter at Hawaii and return to their trading in furs the next spring. It was an ideal place to obtain those fresh supplies of hogs, fowl, fruit, vegetables, cocoanut, and sugar cane which were so welcome to weary seamen after months of salt pork washed down by spruce beer. Furthermore, the islands could supply a useful product to supplement a cargo of skins. The merchants of Canton were always ready to pay a high price for a few piculs of the fragrant sandalwood which Captain Kendrick about 1790 discovered growing wild on the island of Kauai.

With some few exceptions the relations between the Americans and the Hawaiians were extremely friendly. The naturalness of the islanders, and that effervescent spirit which led their first visitors enthusiastically to call them the happiest people in the world, were as welcome a change from the somberness of the Northwest Indians as were the inviting beaches of the islands after America's rocky coast-line. 'The characteristics of these islanders,' wrote Cleveland, 'are activity, gayety, volatility, and irritability; those of the Northwest Indians, heaviness, melancholy, austerity, ferocity, and treachery.'

Unless a taboo should happen to be in effect — one of those periodic *verbotens* by which the native priests exerted their authority and forbade any Hawaiian to go upon the water — the arrival of an American vessel invariably was the signal for an excited descent upon the newcomers. The islanders were ready to barter their fresh supplies for almost anything made of iron, and in the early days of the trade nothing more was needed to replenish a ship's larder than a good supply of knives, hatchets, or even nails.

The most cordial welcome was also extended to the Americans by the islands' ruler, King Tamaamaah.[1] This ambitious potentate was actively extending his power over the whole archipelago during this period and he quickly learned from the visitors certain of the ways of the West which proved helpful in his campaigns in the outlying islands. Their trade brought him firearms and ammunition and no vessel could long remain at anchor before he paid it an official visit and sounded out the prospects of an exchange of sandalwood for weapons of war.

A 'large athletic man, nearly naked,' is one of the first

[1] Tamaamaah, as he was then called, is known to history as King Kamehameha I.

descriptions of this remarkable personage, but he soon paid his visits in greater style. An impressive costume made up of a blue broadcloth coat, a red waistcoat, and velveteen breeches trimmed with red, became his state uniform when he called upon the American captains, stalking proudly about their decks with a long sword clanking at his side. Often he would be accompanied by one or more of his favorite wives, ladies, we are told, who were very beautiful, but of 'unmeasured size.' Sometimes the festivities on shipboard during these visits were quite unrestrained. We read of royal swimming races and of the queens getting very drunk.

After such ceremonies the American sailors hurried ashore, and there is no question that not least among the Hawaiian attractions were the ladies of the realm, however enormous they might be. Knowing none of the conventions of the West, the natives were as glad to lend their wives to the Americans as to each other, and the first mark of Hawaiian hospitality was to offer the travelers their choice among the native women. The 'females were quite amorous,' wrote John Boit, Jr., on one occasion, and in his description of the second visit of Americans to the Sandwich Islands he declared that 'not many of the Columbia's Crew prov'd to be Josephs.'

Under such conditions it is little wonder that only special vigilance on the part of captain and officers could keep most of a ship's crew from deserting the hard life of a sailor for a taste of Hawaiian freedom. Some of them did take up permanent residence ashore, the nucleus of the American colony of later years, and lived there under Tamaamaah's friendly protection. Two of them, John Young and Isaac Davis, became the King's trusted advisers and influential middlemen in the sandalwood trade. Another, Samuel

Patterson, was granted land, servants, and the choice of any women whom he favored except the wives of the chiefs. A friendly haven and a selection of women were also offered one Archibald Campbell, an English sailor from an American ship which had been wrecked on the Northwest Coast.

Unfortunately, the natives beyond the influence of Tamaamaah were not always as friendly as this, and in the early days of the trade precautions sometimes had to be taken more reminiscent of the coast than of the courteous hospitality of 'Owhyhee' itself. Captain Ingraham had a first experience of this sort when the *Hope* was once surrounded by seven hundred canoes with twenty thousand fighting men, and only the quick seizure of hostages averted an attack by these 'very Trecherous and Deceitfull' people.

Another story is told by John Bartlett, who had sailed to Canton on the *Massachusetts* in 1790, and, after its sale by Samuel Shaw, reshipped on a coast voyage on the snow *Gustavus*. When this vessel reached the islands, it followed the custom of the day in entertaining friendly visitors, and one night 'every man in the ship took a girl and sent the remainder ashore.' Suddenly a signal was given, and while 'every Girl in the Ship Clung fast to her Man in a very Loving Maner,' their lawful spouses cut the vessel's anchor ropes. But the seamen acted promptly to prevent their ship from drifting ashore. Breaking away from the affectionate embraces of their companions, they drove the women into the cabin and got the *Gustavus* under sail. The next morning they returned to the scene of the plot, and, after a little skirmishing with the natives, allowed the women to jump overboard and make the best of their way ashore.

Far more serious was the experience of Captain Metcalf and the ill-fated brig *Eleonora*. This New York vessel was one of the first to engage in the Northwest trade — Samuel

Shaw reported her off Macao on his second voyage and in 1789 she was in Nootka Sound — and on one of its voyages Captain Metcalf arranged a rendezvous at the islands with a smaller vessel, the *Fair American*, which he had bought in Macao and placed under the command of his son. No sooner had the *Eleonora* reached the appointed place than one of her crew was murdered by the natives, and, as the story is told, his bones brought back to the ship and offered for sale.

Incensed at this insult and treachery, Captain Metcalf determined on a bloody revenge. He went on peacefully trading and threw handfuls of beads over the side of his ship to draw in as close as possible all the native canoes which were swarming about his vessel. Then without warning he fired a sudden broadside into their midst. Some three hundred Hawaiians were said to have been killed.

But this was not all. All unknown to Captain Metcalf at the time he was carrying out this wholesale execution of the innocent and the guilty, his son's command, the *Fair American*, had been ambushed on another side of the island. Its entire crew, with the exception of one man, was massacred.

How much this bloody stain upon the early relations between the Americans and the Hawaiians may have been due to the way in which Captain Metcalf treated the natives is not known. There is evidence that both in Hawaii and on the Northwest Coast he recognized no scruples in obtaining his fresh supplies or his furs. At all events, he paid the final penalty for his possible mistreatment of the natives, for a few years later the *Eleonora* met much the same fate on the Northwest Coast as that which had overtaken the *Fair American* in Hawaii. Somewhere among the Queen Charlotte Islands the vessel was seized by the Indians and Captain Metcalf and all but one of the crew were killed.

This incident was not in any way typical of the growing intercourse between Americans and Hawaiians. The only real check upon their early trade was due not to treachery on the part of the natives but to their increasing sophistication. After Captain Kendrick had taken the first cargo of sandalwood to Canton on the *Lady Washington*, this adjunct to the fur trade continued to grow and prosper until it, too, was interrupted by the War of 1812. One contract which the Winship brothers of Boston had made with King Tamaamaah for the entire monopoly on all the sandalwood grown in his territories was repudiated, and after the war both the King and his people were more exacting in their demands upon the American traders. The knives and hatchets and nails of the first days of barter were no longer good currency.

When Captain Hill arrived in the *Ophelia* in 1816, he found that all the King wanted was American-made schooners; his chiefs such products of the West as carriages,[1] damask tablecloths, and rum. From the account books of William French, who came out to Hawaii in the brig *Neo* two years later, we find that the demand then was for European clothing, arms, and ammunition. On one day Tamaamaah bought two shirts for a canoe-load of vegetables and a week later sixteen kegs of rum, a box of tea, and eight thousand dollars' worth of guns, powder and shot, paying for this transaction with eight hundred and fifty piculs of sandalwood. The next year his son bought thirty-four

---

[1] Captain Cleveland had brought the first horse to Hawaii in 1803. The people were greatly excited; Tamaamaah blasé. He could not see that a horse's ability to transport a person faster than he could walk was sufficient compensation for all the food the horse would consume.

South America to Canton. Ship Packet

| Bear.s of Land &c | General Remarks | Currents &c |
|---|---|---|

PAGE OF MANUSCRIPT SEA JOURNAL OF SAMUEL HILL

casks of gunpowder, eighty muskets, and a $4160 sloop, for four hundred and sixteen piculs of sandalwood, four hogs, and his note for an unstated sum.

Soon after this the character of the Hawaiian trade changed still more. King Tamaamaah was succeeded in 1820 by King Liholiho and the precautions which had been taken by Tamaamaah to preserve the sandalwood forests were abandoned. The wood was cut down in such careless haste that it had the double effect of drugging the Canton market with an annual importation of twenty-one thousand piculs and quickly denuding the islands of all sandalwood trees. The Hawaiian Islands were now to become a port for direct trade with the United States, due both to the large numbers of American vessels calling there for supplies [1] and to the growing needs of the Hawaiians themselves, but its days as a way station on the route to Canton were over.

If the islands thus outgrew their part in the China trade, it was nevertheless this trade which first led to American interest in Hawaii, then to the missionary movement which brought the islanders within the pale of Western civilization, and ultimately to annexation.

American seamen rounding Cape Horn and making their way up to the Northwest Coast and then across the Pacific to Hawaii and Canton were not ignorant of the fact that there was a vast intervening coast-line which was part of Spanish America. When sea-otter furs became scarce about Nootka Sound and the mouth of the Columbia, their vessels inevitably crept farther south to California; when weather

---

[1] It was the whalers especially who later made Hawaii a regular port of call. Samuel Eliot Morison says that sixty put into Honolulu in 1822, while some twenty years later the annual arrivals were over four hundred.

or scarcity of provisions made some intermediate halt between the Cape and the Northwest desirable, they did not
hesitate to put into one of the Spanish ports of South
America. But along this entire coast trade with any foreign
vessel was generally forbidden by the Spanish authorities.
Until the establishment of the independence of Mexico and
of the South American Republics, what commerce there
was had to be furtive and contraband. The Americans
traded either with the connivance of the customs guards, or,
should they prove incorruptible, in spite of them.

Along the California coast there were in the days of the
Northwest trade only a few scattered mission stations.
Richard H. Dana was later to paint an unforgettable picture
of the country in 'Two Years Before the Mast,' but before
the trade in hides commenced, California was little known
and American vessels skirting its shore-line were pioneering
in new territory. There were several variations to the trade
they attempted to carry on. The Nor'westmen might try
their luck at such ports as San Diego, San Blas, or Monterey, hoping to find officials willing to place furs in the
category of 'necessary supplies.' They might seek out
Indians on isolated spots along the coast. They might get
in touch with the padres of the mission stations who were
always glad to ignore Spanish regulations and trade for
American goods whatever furs they could obtain from their
Indian converts.

The ship *Otter* of Boston, Captain Ebenezer Dorr, Jr.,
which put into Monterey for 'provisions' in 1796, is believed to be the first American vessel to have anchored in
the waters of California. Four years later another Boston
vessel, the brigantine *Betsy*, Captain Charles Winship, was
ignoring Spanish regulations by trading directly with the
Indians. By 1804 the Americans were annually leaving

some twenty-five thousand dollars in goods and specie along the forbidden coast.

One novel scheme first carried out in this same year was that of Captain Joseph O'Cain in a ship named after himself. By an arrangement with the Russian authorities at New Archangel, he borrowed seventy-five canoes and one hundred and twenty Indians, bringing them with him on a cruise to California. The Indians put off from the ship in their canoes to hunt the sea otter and were so successful that in a single season Captain O'Cain loaded eleven thousand skins.

But the voyage which best gives us a picture of the California trade was that made a few years earlier by Captain Cleveland, soon after those adventures on the Northwest Coast in his fifty-ton cutter. He had returned to Europe in 1801 and there chartered, together with William Shaler, formerly United States Consul-General at Algiers, the brig *Lelia Byrd*. Sailing from Hamburg late that year, they stopped first at Valparaiso, where their relations with the Spanish authorities, suspicious with good reason that their cargo was not directly destined for Canton, soon forced them to proceed farther north. They did not dare enter any other port of Chile or Peru, but at San Blas finally succeeded after considerable intrigue in obtaining permission from the Viceroy of Mexico to exchange a part of their cargo for furs.

They next put into San Diego, but found the commandant of this port unwilling to let them trade on any pretense. Nevertheless, it was arranged to purchase some sea-otter skins from the customs guards without his knowledge. A longboat was sent ashore to collect them and preparations made to put out to sea before such duplicity could be discovered. But the longboat did not return. It had been

seized by the commandant. 'The choice presented us,'
Captain Cleveland wrote, 'was that of submission, indig-
nant treatment and plunder; or resistance and hazarding
the consequences.'

Naturally it did not take a Yankee seaman long to make
up his mind what he should do under such circumstances.
Cleveland promptly went to the rescue of his men, seized
the Spanish soldiers who were holding them prisoners, and
put out to sea. As he passed the fort guarding the entrance
to the harbor, it opened fire. But Cleveland was ready for
the attack. 'As soon as we were abreast the fort,' he wrote,
'we opened upon them, and in ten minutes silenced their
battery and drove everybody out of it. They fired only
two guns after we began, and only six of their shots counted,
one of which went through between wind and water; the
others cutting the rigging and sails. As soon as we were
clear we landed the guard, who had been in great tribulation
lest we should carry them off.'

It was outright, unashamed smuggling, and if the 'battle
of San Diego' does not reflect too highly upon the methods
of American traders on the California coast, it affords a
striking example of their relations with the Spanish. They
had no hesitation in defying constituted authority as long
as they could get away with it.[1] They had no compunctions
about employing all the trickery or force at their command
to make off with the coveted furs which priests, soldiers, or
traders were only too glad to sell them if the arm of the law
could be avoided. Cleveland excused his smuggling on the
ground that the people welcomed it and were oppressed by

---

[1] The author of *Two Years Before the Mast* found Cleveland's fame still
bright when he visited the California coast. 'We take this opportunity to
assure the author,' Dana wrote in a review of Cleveland's book, 'that, after the
lapse of more than thirty years, the story [of his battle] was yet current in San
Diego and the neighboring ports and missions.'

their rulers. To add insult to injury he lost no opportunity wherever he was along the coast of Spanish America to urge the people to follow the example of the United States and throw off the Spanish yoke. Behind him from Valparaiso to San Diego, he left a trail of copies of the American Declaration of Independence.

Another aspect of Cleveland's activities in California is to be found in his experiences upon his next stop in the Bay of San Quintin. Here the *Lelia Byrd* was visited by the padres of the missions of San Vincente, San Domingo, San Rosario, and San Fernando, who arrived on horseback with large retinues of Indian servants. They were a 'jolly set of fellows,' Cleveland wrote. 'Their object seemed to be principally recreation, though they brought a few sea-otters' skins, which they bartered with us for European manufactures.'

Apparently neither race nor religion set up any barriers to the mutual enjoyment these two different sets of men — Yankee seamen and Spanish priests — found in each other's company. The padres had come prepared to stay far longer than their trade could possibly have demanded, and after pitching their tents near the *Lelia Byrd's* anchorage they insisted upon Cleveland's accepting their hospitality. The American sea captain declared that 'never was there an equal number of men more disposed to promote harmony and good fellowship, and we dined together alternately on shore and on board, during the week that they remained with us.'

Thanks to his defiance of the Spanish port authorities and his friendship with the mission fathers, Cleveland was able to secure a full cargo of furs before he left California for Hawaii and Canton. He had made a successful voyage, and by the time he reached Boston and sold his return cargo of tea and silks, his profits were tremendous. He had first sailed to the East in 1797 in a cutter which he bought, together with its cargo, for seven thousand dollars. When eight years later he at last returned home, this original investment had swollen to seventy thousand dollars, for those days a comfortable fortune.

Trade at the ports of Spanish America south of those in California has been described in the remarkable sea journals of Captain Samuel Hill. This New England sailor had a stormy career, sailing first to the Pacific on the *John Jay* in 1795, and in subsequent years voyaging to Japan, in the employ of the Dutch, and to the Northwest Coast, where he was once captured by the Indians. While in Canton on one of these voyages, he came under the influence of the famous missionary, Dr. Robert Morrison, and was persuaded to live a more sober and religious life than that to which he was accustomed as a hard-driving sea captain. It is to this we owe his careful record of his later voyages. It summons up a pleasant picture to imagine Captain Hill forswearing his daily grog and retiring quietly to his cabin to write out in his beautifully clear hand a journal, half nautical observations, and half sad regrets for the follies of his earlier days.

It was in 1815 that he sailed for South America in command of the ship *Ophelia*, three hundred and sixty tons, owned by Perkins and Company of Boston. His cargo was seventy thousand dollars in Spanish silver, which was to be exchanged at Valparaiso for pig copper, this commodity to be taken in turn to Canton and traded for tea and silk.

Captain Hill was accorded a wide discretion by the vessel's owners as to what he should do if it proved impossible to trade at Valparaiso. There were whales' teeth at the Galapagos Islands, sandalwood at Ingraham's Islands, or sea-otter skins at Norfolk Sound. If necessary, he was to stop at Hawaii for sandalwood. Should all these markets fail, he was to try at Batavia for freight to Japan or for a cargo of coffee for Boston. In all events he was to be careful of the Spanish *guardacostas* and to speak no ships which he could avoid.

The *Ophelia* was armed with eight six-pounders, fifteen muskets, two blunderbusses, twelve cutlasses, fifteen boarding pikes, two pairs of pistols, and four hundred rounds of powder and shot. It was estimated that the voyage would take eighteen months, and supplies of bread, beef, and pork for this period were taken aboard. There were twenty-two in the crew, the wages of the able seamen being seventeen dollars a month, and those of green hands and boys from six dollars to ten dollars. Captain Hill had the privilege of ten tons on the home cargo and various commissions on what he bought and sold of from five to seven per cent.

He was a strict disciplinarian, the journal shows us. For sleeping on their watch his seamen were sent to the masthead for two hours and deprived of their grog for two days. There was to be no swearing, blaspheming, or obscene language, and Captain Hill supplemented his attempts to promote godliness, a matter not altogether in his control, by strictly enforcing a cleanliness which did fall within his province. On Saturdays all bedding was to be aired and clothes washed. Sunday was a day of rest, but the men were mustered and had to be clean.

The *Ophelia* met its first adventures after leaving Boston while rounding Cape Horn. Encountering unusually bad weather, two weeks were spent in making the stormy passage between the Atlantic and the Pacific.

'We were scourged with a series of dreadful Gales during which time we had but few Intervals of Moderate Weather and those were Very Short,' wrote Captain Hill. 'The

Winds Varied generally from S.W. to N.W. and sometimes to N.N.W. but the heaviest of these winds was from the West by North and N.W. The terribly heavy Sea, Produced by such a continuation of Gales, operating upon an Ocean, Open even to the Pole, without Interruption except from the Masses of Ice, may readily be conceived. I think I have never seen so heavy a Sea before. With these Gales we wore and tacked occasionally as the wind shifted a few Points, but the drift occasioned by the Current and heave of the Sea, was such that although we carried all the Canvas we Possibly could and never hove to, yet we were enabled to do but little more than keep our Position. The Ophelia Proved a Most Excellent Sea Boat, and Safe Ship, or we should not have done so well, and I considered ourselves as being extremely fortunate in having Suffered no damage, except a Main top Sail split and a jib boom partially sprung....'

Finally, one hundred and twenty-two days out of Boston the battered vessel made Valparaiso. But the Spanish authorities were in an unfriendly mood. There was no disposition on their part to stretch the regulations which allowed foreign ships to obtain fresh provisions into permission to buy any copper, and the *Ophelia* was unable either to trade legitimately or to smuggle. It left port after a brief stay with its cargo of silver dollars still intact.

Ill-luck now continued to dog Captain Hill as he vainly sought out various ports of the Pacific where his specie might be exchanged for some other commodity which could be traded at Canton. At the Galapagos Islands rough weather prevented him from landing even a boat's crew, and at Hawaii there was a temporary feud on between King Tamaamaah and the Americans which prevented him from buying a single picul of sandalwood. The *Ophelia* was

forced to turn westward and, crossing the Pacific by way of
New Britain, the Admiralty Islands — where for a time the
ship was stuck upon a reef — and New Guinea, it at length
reached Batavia. Here again there was no trade for an
American vessel, and Captain Hill continued on the course
to his ultimate goal of Canton. It was August, 1816, when
the *Ophelia* anchored at Whampoa with the exact same
cargo with which it had left Boston a little over a year
before.

The hong merchants could, of course, always use specie
and the voyage was by no means a loss. A cargo of Canton
goods was taken aboard and Captain Hill set out on the
homeward voyage by way of the Cape of Good Hope.
Five months later and the *Ophelia* was in Boston Harbor.

The ill-luck of his ventures in South America, however,
had by no means discouraged Captain Hill with the prospects of trade in the Spanish colonies. Soon after his return with the *Ophelia*, he set out once again for Valparaiso
aboard the *Packet*, two hundred and eighty tons, carrying
a miscellaneous cargo costing some two hundred thousand
dollars.

When he reached the Chilean port on this voyage, it was
to find the South American colonies in open insurrection
and a patriot squadron harassing the regular Spanish shipping. Consequently the authorities eagerly welcomed an
American ship bringing supplies which they could not
import themselves. Free permission was granted Captain
Hill to trade and to export copper, and by sending some of
his goods overland from Valparaiso to Santiago he managed
to do a thriving business.

When he reached Canton with his new cargo, mostly
copper, he found such a ready sale for it that he freighted to
Boston the China goods for which it was exchanged and

returned in the *Packet* to South America. For the next few years he traded regularly back and forth between Canton and Valparaiso, repeating the success of his first venture, and it was not until 1822 that the *Packet* returned to Boston after a total voyage of almost five years.

This Canton–South American trade, in which Captain Hill was by no means the only voyager, never assumed the importance of other branches of America's commerce with China. In 1819, we find that American vessels exported from Canton to South America only $262,830 worth of goods. This seems to be a fair average for the period and an indication of the extent of the direct trade, even though it does not take into account South American products which were picked up *en route* by the fur-traders. But, at the same time, Canton exports to Europe in American ships were six times this amount, and the value of those goods taken directly to the United States twenty-four times as great. It was a trade important only because it represented a phase of that widespread search on the part of the Americans for any products which could be exchanged for Canton's teas and silks.

# CHAPTER VI

## THE SEAL FISHERIES

WHILE American vessels, largely those of Boston, were bartering with the Northwest Indians, establishing an American outpost in Hawaii, and carrying on a furtive contraband trade with Spanish America, Yankee enterprise had simultaneously developed another unexpected and rich source to supply the Canton market with furs. On the barren islands off the coast of Patagonia, in the waters south of Cape Horn, and along the Chilean coast, were discovered vast herds of fur seals. Here, ready at hand — for nothing more was necessary than to club the helpless animals over the head and strip them of their skins — was a product which the Chinese merchants bought as eagerly as they did the fur of the sea otter.

For a period which roughly corresponds with that of the Northwest trade, from about 1790 to 1812, this parallel commerce in the South Atlantic and South Pacific thrived and prospered. Sealskins were taken to Canton by the hundred thousand. Then inevitably the sources of supply became exhausted. Herds which had been estimated to number millions completely disappeared as the sealers methodically and indiscriminately massacred their prey. The southern fur seal shared the fate of the Northwest sea otter, but not before the trade had enriched many a seaman and merchant of the Atlantic ports.

The value of the seal furs to the hong merchants of Canton had been discovered in an indirect and curious way. About the time the *Empress of China* was opening the trade with the East, an Englishwoman, living in Boston, and

widely known as Lady Haley, had dispatched the ship
*States* to the Falkland Islands for hair sealskins and sea-
elephant oil.[1] In collecting their cargo the crew of this vessel also killed some thirteen thousand fur seals and brought
their skins to New York.

There was so little demand for these unknown furs in
American society that they fetched only fifty cents apiece.
It was decided to ship them to the Orient in the hope of
getting a better price for them. Captain Metcalf of the
*Eleonora* carried them out to Canton and, to what must
have been his surprise and gratification, they sold there at
the rate of five dollars per skin, just ten times the price paid
in New York.

Some years passed before this lead was followed by a
direct sealing voyage to Canton, but Elijah Austin, of New
Haven, sent out two ships in 1790 under Captain Daniel
Greene to the Falklands and South Georgia, and in the
same year the ship *Industry* sailed from Philadelphia under
Captain Patten and collected fifty-six hundred skins at
Tristan da Cunha. It proved to be so easy to obtain a full
cargo, and so eager were the Chinese merchants to buy the
skins, that the next few years saw a sudden rush upon the
lonely and inhospitable islands which the seals chose for
their breeding-places.

During the next two decades American vessels, and
especially those of Connecticut, were gathered every year
by the dozen on the rocky shores of the Falklands, Staten
Island, South Georgia, the Aucklands, and especially
Masafuera, one of the Juan Fernandez group, where on a
neighboring isle the original Robinson Crusoe had once

[1] Lady Haley was a sister of John Wilkes, the spectacular English reformer
and arch foe of George III, and of Commodore Charles Wilkes, the American
explorer.

A SEAL ROOKERY IN THE FALKLAND ISLANDS

walked the lonely beach watching vainly for a sail.[1] Captain Benjamin Morrell estimated that from Masafuera alone some three and a half million furs were taken to Canton between 1793 and 1807, while Amasa Delano declared that for the briefer period from 1797 to 1804 the total was three million.

The profits on these voyages were tremendous. The price of the skins fluctuated widely, falling at one time from the original five dollars to as low as thirty-five cents, but around two or three dollars was a fairer average. In 1793, Captain William Stewart in the *Eliza* could get only $16,000 for thirty-eight thousand skins, less than forty-five cents apiece, and, unable to fill his ship with his own China goods, had to carry freight for others to Ostend. Three years later, Ebenezer Townsend, Jr., supercargo of the New Haven ship *Neptune*, sold eighty thousand furs at three dollars apiece. When this latter vessel's return cargo was auctioned, it brought $280,000, a net profit of $100,000 for the owners, $50,000 for the supercargo, and $70,000 for captain and crew.

About the same time as the *Neptune's* voyage, Captain Edmund Fanning made an expedition in the *Betsy* in which the original investment of $7867 mounted to $120,000. After deducting all duties, shares of captain and crew, and capital, this represented a clear profit of $53,118. The

[1] With some appreciation of the hardships Selkirk had undergone, the literary sealers of this period thought little of Defoe for the way he was reputed to have treated the unfortunate sailor. Amasa Delano wrote: 'The amanuensis privately took minutes from Selkirk's journal, and returned the book; telling him, that he could not make any thing of it. Shortly after, this same person had the injustice to avail himself of the hard-earned labours of Selkirk, by the publication of his journal, under the title of the *History of Robinson Crusoe*, the poor man being thus robbed of the only advantage he hoped to reap from his sufferings, and at a period of life when he was so much in need. When we reflect on a transaction like this, we involuntarily exclaim, how can man be thus destitute of feeling for his brother!'

*Concord*, which sailed in 1799, had cost $13,680 and the expenses of its voyage were $11,462. When ship and cargo were auctioned upon its return, they brought $67,794.56.

Only the chance of such generous profits could have induced merchants or seamen to undertake the sealing voyages. They usually lasted from two to three years and for the seamen meant indescribable hardship and discomfort. Most of the voyage was spent at anchor off some cold and barren island, where the shore gangs were busy day after day killing the seals, stripping them of their skins, scraping off the blubber, and pegging out the furs for curing either by sun or salt. It was work which required a certain measure of skill, perhaps, for Nathaniel Appleton in his journal of the ship *Concord's* voyage speaks of the slow progress they made because all hands were green, but it was a brutal and disgusting task.

A hint of this is given in the account by George Staunton, who sailed with the Macartney Embassy to China in 1793, of conditions on the island of Amsterdam, where he found some Frenchmen and Americans left to gather furs while their vessel had gone on to the Northwest Coast. Four men were able to kill and skin one hundred seals a day, but this left them no time to do anything with the dead bodies. They were left to rot. 'A shocking spectacle,' Staunton wrote, 'was thus exhibited at every step, while the smell infected the atmosphere around.'

Sometimes the sealing gangs were left a year or more under such conditions, living in rude huts and getting most of their food by shooting wild hogs, goats, geese, and wild fowl, which they cooked over fires of seal fat. It was not considered necessary to provide them with anything but bread, molasses, and coffee, but they were encouraged to plant vegetable gardens which might in time add potatoes, onions, radishes, or lettuce to their meager diet. Life in the little colonies which sprang up among the various islands of the South Pacific and South Atlantic was rough and hard. Its sole end and aim was slaughter.

The crews of the sealers sailed on shares, but despite this interest in the success of their voyage in no other branch of the China trade were mutiny and desertion so common. Sometimes the sailors gave up their share in the profits to become what were known as 'alone men,' who killed and skinned on their own account in order to sell their furs to the next vessel which touched at the island on which they had been left. Sometimes they found themselves marooned by no choice of their own with little chance of a vessel calling for them for years. Sometimes they were imprisoned by the Spanish, who occasionally awoke to a realization that the seal islands were Spanish territory and the Americans without rights in their profitable trade.

One fascinating story of being marooned is that of Charles H. Barnard, master of the *Nanina*, who spent two years on the Falkland Islands when the crew of a wrecked English ship rewarded the aid he extended to them by running off with his own vessel. He and four companions were left destitute in a bitterly cold climate and their efforts to build a house, to find fuel for their fire, to kill wild hogs for food and sea lions for skin clothes, marked a bitter struggle for life which only ended with the welcome arrival of two British whaling ships.

If the sealers escaped some of the dangers which beset the Northwest traders, for there were no natives lying in wait to seize their vessels, there was one new hazard they had to face. This was the risk involved in attempting to reach the rocky shores or high cliffs which the seals chose for their rookeries. Many a whaleboat was swamped endeavoring to fight its way through the high surf and many seamen were drowned or crushed against the treacherous ledges on which the pounding waves swept their capsized craft.

A typical sealing voyage of the early period was that of the New Haven ship *Neptune*. This was a three-hundred-and-fifty-ton vessel with a crew of forty-five, quite large for a sealer, as one of Delano's vessels which made a voyage of five years was only sixty-two tons. Captain Daniel Greene, who had made the first direct sealing voyage to Canton in 1790, was in command.

Sailing from New Haven in 1796, the *Neptune* first stopped at the Falkland Islands. There a sealing gang was left with a thirty-ton shallop made by the ship's carpenter, and Captain Greene went on to the Patagonian coast. The Spanish protested against their activities on the mainland, but when they put a number of the crew under arrest, the Americans promptly broke out of jail, drove off the soldiers who were holding their ship, and calmly sailed away.

A few adventures of this kind and the *Neptune* returned to the Falklands to pick up the men who had been left there and the thirty thousand sealskins they had succeeded in collecting. Captain Greene then debated whether to proceed to Canton by way of the Cape of Good Hope or Cape Horn. Deciding on the latter course, his ship had to beat its way to the Pacific in such bitter weather that her decks were filled with snow and her rigging loaded with ice.

Their next stop was Masafuera, where a number of American ships had already preceded them. The *Neptune's* sealing gang gave a good account of itself despite this rivalry, and within seven weeks fifteen thousand more skins were added to those collected at the Falklands and in Patagonia. This meant a full cargo, and leaving behind twelve men who were to be picked up upon another voyage, the *Neptune* set out across the Pacific.

After a brief stop at Hawaii — for the sealers as well as the Nor'westmen were apt to break their voyage at these friendly islands — they reached Canton and exchanged their furs for tea, some twelve hundred chests of Bohea and smaller quantities of Hyson, Hyson Skin, and Souchong. Then the voyage home through the Straits of Malacca, past Penang, Mauritius, and the Cape of Good Hope, until, on July 11, 1799, after having been away almost three years, the *Neptune* sighted New Haven harbor. The profits of this venture, as we have already seen, brought a small fortune to its promoters.

At Masafuera the *Neptune* had met Captain Fanning and the *Betsy*. This redoubtable sailor was more closely identified with the sealing trade than any other merchant-captain of his day and it is reputed that he was either captain or directive agent of seventy voyages to the South Seas and China. Born at Stonington, Connecticut, in 1769, he first went to sea when he was fourteen. Fifty-seven years later, at the age of seventy-one, he was still active, memorializing the Government in favor of an exploring and trading expedition to discover new seal islands in the Antarctic.

His voyage in the *Betsy* was one of his most memorable ventures. Like the *Neptune*, this vessel first stopped at Patagonia and the Falkland Islands, where the crew had more success in hunting wild hogs through the tussock bogs than in killing seals, and then went on to Masafuera. Here one of their whaleboats was capsized in the surf and another stove into pieces, but in ten weeks from January to April the sailors killed so many seals that even the cabin and forecastle of the *Betsy* were filled with skins. And at that four thousand more were left ashore in charge of a boat's crew.

Setting out for Canton, the next halt was made, not at the Hawaiian Islands, but at the Marquesas. At Nukahiva, one of the Washington group which had been discovered by Captain Ingraham in the *Hope*, the most friendly relations were established with the natives. They surrounded the *Betsy*, 'much like a flock of blackbirds upon a tree,' and eagerly exchanged breadfruit, yams, cocoanuts, bananas, and sugar cane for Captain Fanning's trading supply of hatchets, chisels, buttons, beads, and looking-glasses. A formal visit was paid to the native king and he was ceremoniously presented with a metal plaque, bearing the name of the *Betsy* and its home port, which was hung about his majesty's royal neck with a crimson ribbon. Two hundred ladies of the court, clothed in white and with white turbans, were formally introduced to the Americans. It was a ceremony which the startled travelers soon discovered meant rubbing noses with every one of the native women.

After leaving Nukahiva, the *Betsy's* next stop was at the Ladrone Islands, where Fanning rescued the crew, including the captain's wife and daughter, of a wrecked English ship, and then proceeded to Canton. This friendly act caused complications. The Chinese would let no females land — 'it no have China custom; how can do?' — and not until the East India Company had intervened and bribed the officials could Captain Fanning get rid of his awkward guests and obtain permission to sell his cargo. Once this was done, little time was lost in loading the *Betsy* with China goods and sailing for New York. After an uneventful crossing of the Indian Ocean and the Atlantic, the home port was reached on April 26, 1799.

Captain Fanning was soon at sea again and in search of new seal herds. This time he sailed in the letter-of-marque *Aspasia* and penetrated as far into the south as the island of South Georgia. It was mid-winter when he arrived and the temperature was thirty-six degrees below zero. His ship became coated with ice and almost heeled over while his men landed on an iceberg to lay the keel of a thirty-ton shallop. Before the season commenced, the *Aspasia* was joined by seventeen other sail, but so expert were its crew that, of the one hundred and twelve thousand skins taken off the island that year, they accounted for fifty-seven thousand.

Another of Fanning's ships, the *Catherine*, commanded by his brother, Captain Henry Fanning (there were eight boys in the family, all of whom went to sea), a few years later found a new source for sealskins in the Indian Ocean. It had become necessary by this time (1805) to go farther and farther afield to get a full cargo of furs for Canton. The seals on the islands off South America were becoming scarce, and two years earlier Joel Root, supercargo of the New Haven ship *Huron*, had reported that at Masafuera there were almost as many sealers as seals. Some one hundred and fifty men from American vessels were fighting for the depleted herd, and the crew of the *Huron* were able to obtain only four thousand skins themselves and to buy ten thousand more from the 'alone men.'

Henry Fanning's find was the rediscovery of the Crozet Islands. Two seasons were spent searching for them, and it was a glorious day when their shores were at last sighted and found to be covered with thousands of seals. The *Catherine* paid a quick visit to Prince Edward Island, where a note was hidden to tell another of the Fanning ships of the marvelous discovery, and then returned to the Crozets, where a full cargo for Canton was soon taken aboard.

On another search for seals in 1808, Captain Mayhew Folger, of the Boston ship *Topaz*, decided to try his luck at

Pitcairn Island in the hope that it might have an untouched rookery. As he approached the island, a double canoe filled with natives put out to meet the ship, and to the amazement of Captain Folger the *Topaz* was hailed in perfectly good English.

When the islanders came aboard, it soon developed that they were not full-blooded natives, but the children of the mutineers of the *Bounty*, an English ship which had completely disappeared some twenty years before after its commander, Lieutenant William Bligh, of the British Navy, had been set adrift with a few of his crew while on a voyage carrying breadfruit from Tahiti to the West Indies. Only one actual survivor of the mutiny was left on Pitcairn Island, a man named Alexander Smith, and it was an amazing story which Captain Folger now heard from him and later communicated to the British Admiralty.

After the mutiny, the *Bounty* had returned to Tahiti. A few of the crew had remained — later to be arrested and court-martialed in England — while the rest put out to sea again under the command of one Fletcher Christian, taking with them a number of Polynesian men and women. They landed at Pitcairn Island, deserted and little known, promptly burned their ship, and founded a settlement. It was made up of eight Englishmen and the six men and twelve women whom they had brought from Tahiti.

For a time all went well, but after the death of Fletcher Christian the trouble began. The Tahitians grew jealous and discontented, until one day, without warning, they seized their arms and massacred every surviving Englishman except Alexander Smith. Then the very night following this massacre, the Tahitian women took a bloody revenge for the murder of the whites. They killed every single Tahitian man. When Captain Folger appeared, there was left on this lonely island in the Pacific a group of thirty-four women and children over whom Alexander Smith presided as sole survivor of the English fugitives.

Not a single vessel had called at Pitcairn Island until the arrival of the *Topaz*, but the patriarch of the little community had brought up his flock as English men and women. He had instructed them especially in the Christian religion, and one of Captain Folger's greatest surprises, when he invited some of these supposed natives to dine on his ship, was their insistence upon saying grace before starting the meal.

The *Topaz* left the community as it had found it, and in the course of the next few years it was visited by several other vessels, both English and American. Finally, in 1830, a British ship removed the colony to Tahiti, as Pitcairn Island was suffering from drought, and then once again its strange history became entangled with that of the China trade. The descendants of the *Bounty* mutineers did not take kindly to Tahiti, and the next year Captain William Driver, of the Salem ship *Charles Doggett*, agreed to take them all back to Pitcairn Island. He collected as pay from his sixty-five passengers some old copper, twelve blankets, and one hundred and twenty-nine dollars in missionary drafts.[1]

To return again to the sealers themselves. The gradual extinction of the herds, not only on the Falklands and at Masafuera, but also at South Georgia and the Crozet Islands, had made the old voyages unprofitable by the time of the War of 1812. The importation of the furs at Canton had fallen from several hundred thousand a year to

---

[1] The descendants of the mutineers of the *Bounty* still live on Pitcairn Island. The latest count puts their number at one hundred and forty. They are Seventh Day Adventists, grow coffee, and keep poultry and goats.

a few score thousand, and the seal trade was gradually dying out just as was that in the furs of the sea otter. But about 1819 it had a sudden, brief revival, and although in this period it was more common to bring the skins back to the United States than to carry them directly to Canton, a chapter on the seal fisheries cannot close without mention of the days of glory of the port of Stonington.

It was from this little Connecticut port that Captain Fanning had directed so many of his voyages and at one time it had a sealing fleet of twelve small vessels totaling eight hundred and fifty tons and carrying two hundred and two men. From it there sailed in 1819 the *Hersilia*, commanded by Captain James P. Sheffield and with William A. Fanning as supercargo, on an expedition to sail as far south as possible in the hope of discovering land beyond any then known to Americans.

Making its dangerous way ever farther into the misty region of snow and ice below Cape Horn, the *Hersilia* came upon the South Shetlands. Their shores were thick with seals. Captain Sheffield killed and skinned eleven thousand — he could have taken fifty thousand, he later reported — and hurried back to Stonington with his precious secret.

Amid much excitement and mystery, preparations were made for a second expedition. It was pretended that whaling and not sealing was the object of the intended voyage, but the secret could not have been very well kept. For in 'Niles' Register,' published in Baltimore, there was a notice in 1820 of a Stonington ship being outfitted for 'an island unknown to any one except the captain, where seals which had never been disturbed by man, were tame as kittens, and more plentiful than at any other place upon earth.'

Five vessels left in the Stonington fleet that year. Arriving at the South Shetlands, some one hundred and fifty thousand skins were taken aboard within a few weeks. And while this work of killing and skinning was going on so rapidly, one little vessel slipped away to make a further discovery, which is still known as Palmer Land, a perpetual reminder of how far into the Antarctic the Connecticut sailors dared to penetrate. The man from whom this name derived, Captain Nathaniel B. Palmer, was then only twenty-one, and his command a tiny sloop called the *Hero*, 'but little rising forty tons.'

No more seals were found on the ice-bound coast of Palmer Land, however, and those on the South Shetlands could not long outlast the slaughter of Stonington's annual fleet. The fur seals were killed here as they had been everywhere else and even the Antarctic could yield no further riches to carry to Canton.

# CHAPTER VII

## ISLANDS OF THE SOUTH SEAS

THE charms of the South Sea Islands have had a special vogue in our generation. The lazy delight of life on some Pacific isle, where the long rollers break on palm-fringed shores and obliging monkeys toss cocoanuts and mangosteens to world-weary travelers, has been sung again and again. But it is not the twentieth century which discovered the South Seas. In their continual voyaging in search of new products to carry to Canton, the pioneers of our commerce with the Far East came to know them well, and there was scarcely an island in all the Pacific which was not visited by an American vessel in the development of the China trade of a century and more ago.

The Marquesas were well known in the eighteenth century. Ingraham had touched there as early as 1791 and given such good American names as Washington, Adams, Lincoln, Knox, Franklin, Hancock, and Federal to the outlying group he had discovered to the northwest. Fanning had followed his trail, and a little island midway between Hawaii and the Society Islands still bears his name as a monument to Yankee ubiquity in the Pacific. The *Concord* also knew the Marquesas, the brig *Franklin* in 1800 called at the Fijis, whose treacherous coral reefs presented 'the most intricate and most dangerous navigation ever undertaken by man,' and three years later Amasa Delano called at Wake Island. The Admiralty Islands, the Caroline Islands, the Friendly Islands, New Guinea, and New Britain were familiar to the early traders. The Philippines were of course known as one of the gateways to Canton, as also Guam, Tahiti, and Samoa. Whether or not they found their place on the official maps, these islands were marked on the charts of American sea captains. Trade did not wait to follow the flag. It did not wait even for formal discovery. It found its own way throughout the Pacific.

The products of these isles which might be expected to appeal to the peculiar tastes of the merchants and mandarins of Canton were many and varied. There was sandalwood which could often be obtained by simple barter with the natives; tortoise-shell and mother of pearl; edible birds' nests, sharks' fins, and *bêche de mer* — a slimy sea slug — which the Chinese prized for their rich soups. No great trade could be expected in such strange commodities, but in the keen competition with the East India Company they offered the Yankees some chance to keep abreast of their rivals. For England's Eastern possessions afforded a source of supply for the Canton market which the Americans had had to discover for themselves.

When conditions were favorable and all went well, this South Sea trade was highly profitable. As with the Indians of the Northwest Coast, all that was necessary to put the natives to work collecting valuable cargoes was an assortment of trinkets and iron tools. Whales' teeth, hatchets and knives made at the ships' forges, glass bottles, calico, needles, nails, and looking-glasses had an invariable appeal for Fiji Islanders or Marquesans.

Sandalwood was often contracted for as at Hawaii, and on at least one occasion, the voyage of the *Hope*, Captain Reuben Brumely, a treaty was ceremoniously signed with a Fiji chief, who agreed not only to collect a full cargo, but to forbid any further trading until either the *Hope* or another vessel sent out by its owners returned. Under direction of the vessel's officers the sandalwood was cut, sawed into lengths, the bark shaved off, and the wood neatly piled on the shore ready to be taken aboard. Its cost came to about one cent a pound; at Canton it was worth thirty-four cents.

When a second vessel of the *Hope's* owners, the ill-fated *Tonquin* which later came to grief on the Northwest Coast, returned to the Fijis, another lot of wood had been similarly prepared and the native chief was impatiently waiting the Americans' arrival. He had taken such a fancy to one of the ship's officers that he had adopted him as his son. We are told in the account of the *Tonquin's* voyage that the American sailor's return deeply affected the romantic islander — 'large, pearly drops rolled down his cheeks, and he was, to all appearances, quite overjoyed, and affectionately unmanned in again meeting with his adopted son!'

For *bêche de mer* and other South Sea products the process of obtaining a cargo was almost as simple as in the case of sandalwood. Sometimes the seamen would gather the sea slugs or the birds' nests themselves, but more often the natives were ready to do so at slight cost. *Bêche de mer* had to be cured by boiling in pothouses on shore, then dried and stowed away in matting bags. This occasionally presented difficulties, but Edmund Fanning tells of one voyage on which he was able within ninety days to secure a cargo which at Canton was sufficient to exchange for a full lading of China goods as well as pay all port charges.

No branch of the Canton trade, however, was without its risks and hazards, and certainly that with the South Sea Islands was no exception. The Fijis especially were a point of danger, not alone because their uncharted reefs and shoals held out the constant menace of running aground, but because not every chief was 'affectionately unmanned' in meeting Americans. The islanders were more likely in

the early days of the trade to think of their visitors as tasty
morsels for a cannibalistic feast, and many Yankee seamen
met a fate which such of their companions as escaped Fiji
treachery did not dare to dwell upon. Among other islands,
and in time even at the Fijis, the American voyages were
made under those idyllic conditions we associate with the
South Seas, but at first every ship which picked its way
among the Fiji coral reefs found itself surrounded night and
day by swarms of native canoes, affording constant evidence, as Captain Fanning wrote, 'that if we should be
wrecked, immediate massacre was the destiny of all on
board.'

One vessel to meet this fate was the brig *Union*. On its
first voyage to the Fijis its captain and a boat's crew had
been killed while ashore and the vessel itself narrowly
escaped capture. On a second visit a heavy squall blew up,
and before the *Union* could get clear into the open sea, it
had been swept upon the reefs and completely wrecked.
Every person on board was either drowned, or, if he succeeded in making his way to land, murdered by the natives.

Some years later, in 1808, the brig *Eliza* and the *Juno*, a
Providence vessel, were also shipwrecked, but in each case
there were survivors. Charles Savage, of the *Eliza*, won the
confidence of the islanders and became a headman at Bau.
A rough-and-tumble foreign community had been established there by shipwrecked or deserting sailors and twenty-
six escaped convicts from New South Wales. Samuel Patterson, of the *Juno*, was made a slave when his vessel was
wrecked, but eventually escaped to tell the story of his
captivity in a pathetic little book published in 1817. Its
title was 'Narrative of the Adventures and Sufferings of
Samuel Patterson, experienced in the Pacific Ocean, and
many other parts of the world, with an account of the Fegee

and Sandwich Islands.' Its authenticity and the deserving
worth of the author were attested by the Reverend Timothy
Merritt, of Wilbraham, and Abel Bliss, Jr., Esq., 'a Literary
and Religious Character of the same place.'

The *Juno* ran upon the rocks off the Fiji coast near midnight of June 20, 1808. Masts and rigging were quickly cut
away, and launching a longboat the crew lay beside their
wreck all night in a high sea. With morning they attempted
to make their way ashore, bringing with them thirty-four
thousand dollars in specie from their ship's cargo. But the
islanders had already learned of the wreck and were massed
to greet the sailors with bows and arrows, spears, and war
clubs. Resistance was hopeless, and so a bargain was struck.
The natives promised the shipwrecked crew their lives in
return for all their possessions, and, after stripping them
even of their clothes, marched them off to a near-by village.
Their fate was to be captivity. Patterson naïvely tells us
that he 'retired to a cocoanut tree, and sat down under it
and gave vent to a flood of tears.'

After a time one of the chiefs took a fancy to the lament-
ing sailor and carried him off to a neighboring island. Patterson promptly became very ill, and being of little use to
his captor under such conditions was left to lie in forlorn
nakedness in an old house used for storing yams. He was
given practically nothing to eat, and whenever it rained he
found himself half buried in the mud. Occasionally the
natives would pay him a friendly visit, carefully feeling his
legs with the comforting comment of 'peppa longa sar
percolor en deeni' — 'white man, you are good to eat.'

For five weeks he endured this life, until one day, feeling
somewhat recovered, he found a canoe and attempted to
escape. It leaked so badly that he had to turn back and was
almost killed by the natives when they learned of his

escapade. He was thrown into his shed again and for three weeks more lay ill. Despairing of freedom, he was so 'awfully tempted with the devil' that he wanted to end his agony. Putting a piece of bark about his neck he tried to hang himself. He was too weak.

Sometime after this experience, when Patterson had again somewhat recovered his health, he was taken back to the island on which the *Juno* had been wrecked. Here he discovered a canoe and for the second time attempted to escape. The first sail he sighted disappeared into the distance before he could catch up with it, and he almost lost his canoe, but finally his luck turned. He happened upon the English brig *Favorite*, of Port Jackson, and was safely taken aboard. Patterson had lost the use of his legs as one price of his captivity, he was half dead from fatigue and almost starved, but when the English sailors gave him a chew of tobacco and a drink of grog, he tells us that he thought himself in heaven.

The *Tonquin*, Captain Brumely, being then at the Fijis taking on its load of sandalwood, the survivor of the *Juno* was transferred to this American vessel and taken to Canton. Here the United States Consul came to his aid. 'And my heart can never lose a tender affection,' wrote Patterson, 'for his great goodness to me in my bitter affliction.'

If this was the end of his adventures, it was not that of his trials and tribulations. As he was incapacitated for work as a seaman, he could find no one who would take him back to America. Even the captain of the *Ann and Hope*, a Providence vessel belonging to the owners of the *Juno*, refused him passage. Patterson's hopes had sprung high when this vessel put into Canton, and its captain's cruel reply to his request to be taken home went to his heart 'like a naked sword.' It was not until January, 1810, more than a year and a half after the *Juno* had been wrecked, that the stranded sailor at last found a berth on the *Baltic*, Captain Eborn.

'My joy I cannot describe,' Patterson wrote, but in an attempt to do so he burst into poetry, and with these verses we may leave him sailing back to Providence and to the publication of his adventures and sufferings:

> 'I have seen the world abroad,
>  Plow'd the briny ocean road;
>  Now my soul transported chimes,
>  Happy, happy native climes.
>
> 'Now I hope to see again,
>  Long estranged Fredonia's plain;
>  Mortal tongues can never show,
>  Pleasures like to those I know.'

Other wrecks on the Fiji Islands were those of the *Oeno*, a Nantucket vessel, whose entire crew were massacred in 1827, and of the *Glide*, a Salem ship, whose crew were spared as had been the seamen of the *Juno*. The story of the latter has been preserved, but it differs little from that told by Patterson except that the captured sailors were given the protection of a friendly chief. In time they were taken off by the *Harriet*, New York, and the barque *Peru*, Salem.

The grand old man of the South Sea trade seems to have been Benjamin Morrell, a Stonington sea captain who turned to trade in sandalwood and *bêche de mer* after his voyages throughout the Pacific in search of sealskins had proved no longer profitable. In his experiences we get not only a picture of the danger of dealing with treacherous natives, but a first glimpse of those delights of the South

Sea Islands which have given them their popularity to-day.

Morrell sailed for the Pacific in 1829 on board the schooner *Antarctica*, taking his wife with him on the long voyage. This was not an altogether unusual occurrence, but Mrs. Morrell had had difficulties in winning her husband's consent. 'She bathed her pillow with tears at night, and drooped all day like a fading lilly,' the obdurate sea captain tells us, and it was only fear for her health which at last persuaded him to let her accompany him. Perhaps she might better have stayed at home. Sickness and fever marked the voyage until the *Antarctica* took on fresh supplies at the island of Tristan da Cunha, where some time before a Yankee seaman, Jonathan Lambert, of Salem, had set himself up as king and ruled supremely for several years.

The Auckland Islands, New Zealand, and the New Hebrides were all visited on the voyage out, and then, heading for the Philippines, Captain Morrell came upon an unknown group of islands which he named Bergh's Group. Here the natives were instructed to collect *bêche de mer* and mother of pearl, which the *Antarctica* would call for after stopping at Manila. After re-provisioning at the Philippines, this was done, but first the schooner stopped at some other islands, known as Young William's Group, and at a place which in the narrative of the voyage is called Massacre Island.

At the first islands Captain Morrell found the inspiration for some poetic passages on the beauty of the females of the South Seas. Their eyes, he wrote, were 'sparkling like jet beads swimming in liquid enamel!... lips of just the proper thickness for affection's kiss... and I believe that I could have spanned... their naked waists with both my hands... imagination must complete the bewitching portrait: I will only add the shade — their skin was a light copper color.' Perhaps it is needless to add that Mrs. Morrell had been left temporarily in Manila.

But the loveliness of the women did not prevent the men from being cruel and treacherous. The *Antarctica* barely escaped capture at Young William's Group, and at Massacre Island had an even worse experience. Trade for *bêche de mer* was started, and Captain Morrell set up his drying-sheds on the shore, and also a forge where the schooner's armorer might make the iron hoops and axes which the natives sought in exchange for gathering sea slugs. On board ship full precautions were taken against any possible attack. Sentinels were always posted, the men all armed, cannon and swivel-guns loaded with grape and canister, battle lanterns kept at hand, and in the arrow-proof cross-trees men stood to their guns with lighted matches. But all seemed to be friendly. Then one day a shore party was suddenly surrounded by three hundred painted savages with bows and war clubs.

A whaleboat was promptly sent to their rescue, but the natives had surprised the men on shore away from their guns, and in the bitter fight before the boat's arrival it was war clubs against cutlasses. Fourteen of the twenty-one men on shore fell before the attack, and of the seven who fought their way to the whaleboat as it landed in the surf, four were badly wounded and the others almost overcome by exhaustion. They put back to their ship, but the natives as quickly jumped into their canoes and followed the retreating Americans with showers of arrows. Not until the whaleboat came within range of the *Antarctica's* guns could the natives be driven off, and even then Captain Morrell did not know whether he could save the ship if an attack was made in force.

As there was no wind and the schooner lay becalmed,

nothing could be done but prepare for every emergency. Orders were given that should the natives gain the deck, the magazine should be fired. Fortunately things did not reach this extremity. The natives returned to shore, and instead of fighting off an attack, the crew of the *Antarctica* had the even more harrowing experience of lying becalmed and helpless while they watched the natives roasting before immense fires the flesh of those of their companions who had been killed on shore.

Captain Morrell could not revenge the death of his men with such a weakened crew, but returning to the Philippines he added a force of Manilamen to the nineteen surviving Americans and immediately returned. This time he anchored off the native village and without waiting opened a general attack with full fire of all the cannon, swivel-guns, and muskets which the *Antarctica* commanded. Ten minutes of this cannonade and the village was leveled. One lone survivor of the first attack was rescued, a man named Leonard Shaw, who had seen the cannibals eating the flesh of his companions and himself been tortured and half-starved, expecting hourly to be roasted in his turn.

It seems almost impossible to believe, but an attempt was then made to renew the trade which had met such a tragic interruption. An improvised fortress was built on shore, and with that protection the seamen once again began to collect *bêche de mer* and to cure it in their drying-sheds. But they were constantly harassed by the natives and had to be on continual guard. The work could not go on successfully, and at last Captain Morrell admitted himself defeated and gave up all hope of collecting a cargo.

For a while he continued to cruise about the South Seas and discovered some new islands which he felt confident would yield the products he sought for the Canton market.

For some reason, however, he made no attempt at this
time to open trade, but instead returned to America. With
him he took two natives, called Sunday and Monday, as
proof of his mysterious discovery, and in a few years he had
persuaded some New York merchants to put him in command of another venture to the Far Pacific.

His new ship was the *Margaret Oakley*, which sailed from
New York in 1834. It carried as a special passenger
Thomas Jefferson Jacobs, whose account of Captain Morrell's adventures takes up the story where Morrell himself
leaves off.

When the *Margaret Oakley* reached tropical Australasia,
its captain became secretive and mysterious. No one should
know the bearings of his islands and all the ship's nautical
instruments were carefully locked up to prevent any of the
officers or crew from taking observations. When they at
last came upon the first of them, it was the isle of dreams,
whether of the nineteenth century or the twentieth.

'Not a sound broke the solemn stillness,' Jacobs wrote,
'save the murmuring of the surf upon the beach and the
carolling of birds among the verdure of the paradisaical
garden that almost hung over the vessel, shading us with
its dense and lofty foliage.' The trade winds were cool and
invigorating; the pure, transparent waters of the lagoons
flashed with fish; tropical fruits grew in abundance, falling into the hands of the happy sailors; and the friendly
natives, freed of all artificial restraints and knowing no
wants, led lives which were a continual round of enjoyment.

'Who would change such a life,' asked Jacobs, 'for the
toils, and cares, and constant miseries of a moneyed slave?'
This was in 1844.

It was a life which Captain Morrell at least could not
resist very well. He seems to have forgotten all about the

owners of the *Margaret Oakley* and to have cruised happily and leisurely about his new-found islands. It was many months before he managed to collect a cargo and carry out his original plans of going to Canton. But once in that port, he called the crew together and regretfully told them that now the romance of the voyage was over, the *Margaret Oakley* was no longer a pleasure ship sailing about the South Seas according to whim and fancy, but a practical, matter-of-fact merchantman.

At this point Jacobs left the vessel to proceed directly home and the *Margaret Oakley* quietly but effectively disappeared. Its owners never learned of its fate and mysterious legends floated about concerning Captain Morrell and the South Sea colony he was supposed to have founded.

They were not quite true. Years later, Jacobs was visited by one of his old shipmates and learned the real story of the fate of the *Margaret Oakley* and its captain. The vessel had not returned to its idyllic islands, but had sailed for home and been wrecked off the coast of Madagascar while most of the crew were ashore. Captain Morrell had accepted this misadventure as the hand of Fate. Without reporting to his owners, he had taken passage on another ship bound back to the South Seas. Somewhere *en route* he died.

# CHAPTER VIII

## CHANGING TRADE

THROUGHOUT this period in which Yankee traders were searching from Nootka Sound to the Fijis for anything and everything which might be sold in the Canton market, the number of American vessels which every year took their place among the shipping anchored at Whampoa naturally increased. In 1784 it was only the *Empress of China* which flew the Stars and Stripes in Chinese waters, but before the end of the century an average of more than ten American voyages a year were converging upon Canton with their varied cargoes of specie, merchandise, sea-otter furs, seal-skins, and sandalwood. From 1804 to 1809 a total of some one hundred and fifty-four vessels found their way to China from the United States. Our trade had completely outdistanced that of France, Holland, Denmark, and Portugal, and we were pressing hard upon the heels of the honorable East India Company.

These ventures into the Pacific had already instilled new life and vigor into American commerce. They had led the way to a stirring revival of mercantile activity from Salem to Baltimore. But the growth of the Canton trade itself, subject to many fluctuations, was unusually irregular. It was not merely that the character of the expeditions to the Northwest and the Seal Islands made a China voyage at best a venturesome risk for merchants and seamen, but, more important, markets for the sale of Canton goods were to a great extent dependent upon conditions in Europe. Like the general commerce of the young republic, the one neutral in a warring world, trade with China flourished with

A VIEW OF WHAMPOA

hostilities among the European states, suffered with peace, and temporarily collapsed with the events of 1812.

The first definite check in its expansion came as a result of the Embargo of 1808. In the following season only eight American vessels reached Canton as compared with thirty-three in the previous season.

One of these ships was John Jacob Astor's *Beaver*. It had slipped out of port, much to the disgust of rival merchants in New York, through a clever ruse which Astor had ingeniously employed to obtain a special sailing permit from President Jefferson. The great fur merchant had won this exceptional privilege by claiming that there was an important Chinese mandarin aboard the *Beaver*. His position was represented as being so influential that it would be extremely impolitic to force him to remain in the United States because of an embargo which had nothing to do with relations with China. Jefferson solemnly considered the case as a question of national comity. At length he wrote that the opportunity of making the United States known to the Chinese 'through one of its own characters of note' made the granting of a passport to the *Beaver* a diplomatic measure 'likely to bring lasting advantages to our merchants and commerce with that country.'

Too late it was disclosed that this important mandarin for whom the President had interceded was simply a coolie member of the *Beaver's* crew. By that time Astor's vessel was well on its voyage.

After the withdrawal of the embargo, the trade to the Far East quickly recovered and flourished gayly until the shadow of war with England. The American imports at Canton varied from three to six million dollars a year, a great part of them specie despite the thousands of seal and otter skins collected at such hazard, while exports to the

United States to an equal amount were in the form of teas, silk, and nankeens. The amount of tea brought to America in the first decade of the nineteenth century, much of it for reshipment to Europe, was almost double that imported in the last decade of the eighteenth.

To the English at Canton this growing trade was becoming more and more a cause of grave anxiety. They had to recognize that little American ships, about a third the size of their East-Indiamen and 'manned by sailors of exceptional alertness of mind and body,' were undermining their monopoly. A report to the East India Company at London as early as 1809 spoke of this 'deeply irritating neutral trade.'

Consequently it is not surprising that the troubles of 1812 were preceded by British interference with American shipping in the Far East along exactly the same lines as that experienced by our vessels in other parts of the world. On the plea that the American ships were harboring British deserters, they were searched by British men-of-war and their seamen impressed with absolute effrontery. No respect was paid to the territorial sovereignty which the Chinese were powerless to enforce, and the fact that a ship was anchored in the reaches of Whampoa afforded it no more protection than if it had been on the high seas.

The only way in which the Americans could maintain their rights and hope to keep their crews intact was by the threat of armed resistance. Nor was it an idle threat. Seamen fresh from warding off the attacks of Northwest Indians and natives of the South Sea Islands were more than ready to train their guns upon British boarding parties. The armed ships and fighting sailors of the Pacific were not the peaceful merchantmen of the Atlantic.

In 1807, the resentment of the Americans against impressment became so bitter that affairs reached a crisis. Hostilities were about to break out between the British and Americans. The former had established a virtual blockade of Canton and were threatening to seize every American ship. The latter were ready to defend themselves. Sentries were posted and arms and ammunition served out to every crew.

At this point there might easily have been a naval engagement had not Captain Edmund Fanning, who that year was in command of the *Tonquin*, decided to take the risk of running the blockade. He was stopped by a British vessel and quietly went aboard with his papers to sound out the intentions of the English by a test case. To his own good fortune and to that of all Americans in port, he discovered that he personally knew the British commodore. He was able to explain the position of his countrymen and thanks to his good offices the British decided to lift the blockade. Peace was restored and the interrupted trade continued for a time without any further interference with American shipping.

When actual war between the two countries broke out some five years later, Canton did become the scene of open hostilities. Both British war vessels and American letters-of-marque brought in their captured prizes, and this led to conflicts in which China's territorial rights were completely disregarded, and to a British blockade of the port which only three Boston vessels were able to run. The *Rambler*, the *Jacob Jones*, and the *Tamaamaah* 'escaped dashingly the British blockading squadron' in 1815, but the rest of the American merchant fleet was bottled up.

The most exciting incident in the course of the war occurred when *H.M.S. Doris* took the American ship *Hunter* off the Ladrone Islands, brought her to Whampoa as a prize, and then captured a schooner, after a brief fight in which one Englishman was killed, within ten miles of Canton. This was too much for the American vessels at Whampoa. They decided that such a flagrant disregard of Chinese sovereignty could work both ways. Arming their crews, they went to their countryman's assistance and after a vigorous engagement forced the British to release the American schooner.

On the whole, the China trade was effectively disrupted by the war. While the American shipping at Whampoa lay inactive, the British successfully drove the Yankees off the Northwest Coast and away from Hawaii. Astoria was surrendered and a British sloop forced King Tamaamaah to break his contract with the Winship brothers for the delivery of sandalwood. Britain commanded the Pacific and no American war vessels appeared at Canton to protect the China trade.[1]

Peace, however, brought a revival of the commerce even more spectacular than that which had followed the lifting of Jefferson's embargo. Thirty American vessels reached Canton in the season of 1815–16, thirty-eight the next year, thirty-nine the next, and no less than forty-seven in 1818–19. This set a new mark for the China trade and both the imports and exports were over nine million dollars.

In the Essex Institute at Salem there is a manuscript copy of the returns of American vessels at Canton from June 6, 1816, to May 25, 1817. No other source gives such a clear and concise picture of the China trade at this period when it was recovering from the interruption of war.

Forty-three vessels came into port under the American

[1] One American vessel, the frigate *Essex*, Captain David Porter, cruised about the South Pacific preying upon British commerce with dramatic success, but it never came near enough the China coast to be of any aid to traders from Canton.

flag; thirty-eight left. The smallest of these ships was of one hundred and forty-seven tons burden and the largest four hundred and seventy-nine; the average size still being something less than three hundred tons. Their crews ranged from eleven to thirty and averaged about twenty. Boston was the home port of the greatest number, eleven; Philadelphia of nine, New York of seven, Salem of five, Baltimore of four, Providence of three, Amsterdam of three, and Newburyport of one.

Most of these vessels had sailed directly to Canton, but among the ports at which the others had touched were Amsterdam, Antwerp, Gibraltar, Valparaiso, Sumatra, the Northwest Coast, and Batavia. The destinations of the thirty-eight which left China were: Boston nine, Philadelphia nine, New York six, Amsterdam four, Northern Europe three, the Mediterranean two, Providence two, and one each for Baltimore, the Sandwich Islands, and the Northwest Coast.

As for cargoes, the listed imports were silver dollars, ginseng, opium, quicksilver, lead, betel nut, iron, sea otter, land otter, beaver, fox and seal skins, camlets, ebony, copper, cochineal, steel, brimstone, nutria skins, and sandalwood. The exports were largely tea — Bohea, Congo, Campoy, Souchong, Hyson Skin, Hyson, Young Hyson, Imperial and Tokay — together with cassia, chinaware, camphor, sugar, rhubarb, silks, sewing silk, pepper, sugar, candy, aniseed, saltpeter, nankeens, and white lead.[1]

For one of these ships, the *Lion*, sent out by the New York firm of Minturn and Champlin, we have even fuller details in the papers of its supercargo, William Law. They

[1] The total value of all American imports at Canton in this season is given in other sources as $5,609,600, with exports valued at $5,703,000. American disbursements in port are estimated at $250,000.

show that his vessel's cargo was largely silver specie and that he himself, allowed ten tons privilege in addition to his commission of three per cent on all goods bought and sold in Canton, took out three casks containing nine thousand Spanish dollars and a bale of white foxskins. The return cargo included 360 chests of Young Hyson, 362 of Hyson, 3893 of Hyson Skin, 311 boxes of chinaware, and smaller quantities of sugar, cassia, rattans, chinaware, lacquer, crape hangings, paper, silk, paintings, sweetmeats, gold leaf, ivory counters, brushes, and floor mats. Many of these smaller items represented special commissions for Law's friends who wanted Canton shawls, crapes, scarfs, and chinaware. Among the scattered documents there is one brief note in a very feminine hand formally thanking Mr. Law for the 'very elegant Shawl, and Work Box, as a proof of his devotion they will ever be highly esteemed.'

This examination of the trade after the close of the War of 1812 shows little change from conditions during the first decade of its existence. More ships were involved, but they were of the same type, sailing from the same ports and following the same routes. Imports at Canton were still largely specie, with the Northwest, the Seal Islands, and the South Seas represented by a moderate quantity of furs and sandalwood. Exports were the same as those first carried to the United States by the *Empress of China*.

Nevertheless, the commerce with Canton was actually on the brink of an interesting transformation. Voyages to the Northwest and to the islands about Cape Horn were becoming more and more infrequent, as may be seen in the falling-off in the importations of sea-otter furs and sealskins. The direct route from the Atlantic to Canton instead of circuitous voyages about the world was becoming more the rule. The China trade, in short, was losing its air of romance and excitement, and becoming simply a regular commerce which differed from that in other parts of the world only because of the peculiar conditions which still existed in Canton.

The year 1821, when the United States Treasury first began making its annual reports on American trade with China, may perhaps be taken as the division point between the romantic and prosaic periods. Ships after this date became somewhat larger and faster, but because they no longer had to be so heavily armed, they did not need such large crews. The *Empress of China*, three hundred and sixty tons, had a crew of forty-four and could carry a cargo of only four hundred to four hundred and fifty tons. A vessel of this later period might be six hundred and fifty tons burden, but it needed a crew of only twenty-six and could carry thirteen hundred tons of cargo. Moreover, it could sail in any season and make the trip out to China and back, touching perhaps at Anjer in the Straits of Sunda or at St. Helena, in from nine to twelve months, whereas the *Empress of China* had taken fourteen and a half.

For another thing, supercargoes were being entirely replaced by American firms at Canton, and instead of individual merchants providing the initiative and capital for the voyages, they were being undertaken by large companies. In 1825, it was reported that seven eighths of the China trade was in the hands of four firms: Perkins and Company, of Boston; Archer, of Philadelphia; Jones Oakford and Company, of Philadelphia; and T. H. Smith, of New York.

As for ports, Salem had already lost its early significance; Boston and Philadelphia were soon to dwindle in importance. Baltimore had become more active than Providence. New York dominated the trade and was to become the great center for the distribution of tea. It had been the first to send out a voyage to Canton; it was again to be in the lead during the final phase of the old China trade.

Under these new and more prosaic conditions the trade did not yield such high profits. The average return on investments was estimated at six per cent. Competition became too keen in a market which remained so strictly limited in spite of the ingenuity of the Americans in pandering to the tastes of the Chinese. Bills of exchange on London were to take the place of specie and both domestic and foreign manufactured articles were imported to some extent, but there was nothing which the Americans could carry to China in this period and reap such rich rewards as when they first took out ginseng or the furs of the sea otter and the seal.

Grouping together the years from 1821 to 1841, the final period of the old China trade's full development, we find that between thirty and forty vessels were now arriving in Canton every year from American ports, and that combined exports and imports averaged well over ten million dollars. These figures are as true for the end of the period as for its start. The official exports from China to the United States for the season 1821–22 were valued at $5,242,536; those for 1841–42 at $4,934,645. There were years in between when they were valued at about twice these amounts, but there was no consistent expansion to the trade. While American foreign commerce as a whole increased by leaps and bounds and in 1841 was more than six times what it had been fifty years earlier, trade with Canton had remained practically static after its first dramatic period of rapid growth.[1]

[1] For complete figures on trade at Canton throughout the whole period with which this book deals, and a chart indicating its annual fluctuations, see Appendix.

By the time this point was reached, however, the Americans had achieved one thing which had never been thought possible. It will be remembered that English economists had believed that whatever direction American commerce might take, it could not compete with England in the Far East. 'It would hardly be to the interest of the Americans to go to Canton,' Lord Sheffield had declared, 'because they have no articles to send thither, nor any money.' Yet so completely had this theory been disproved that the American trade had passed that of the East India Company and the British were to be compelled to annul the Company's monopoly and throw the China trade open to all Englishmen in order to compete on equal terms with their Yankee rivals.

As early as 1819 it was brought out in parliamentary reports relative to trade with China and the East Indies that the Americans were beginning to handle a greater commerce than the East India Company. The complete English totals always far exceeded those of the Americans because of the independent trade of the 'country ships' which were allowed under special license to sail between Canton and the ports of India — a lucrative trade based upon opium; but in the season of 1817–18 the Company's imports at Canton were $5,045,000 as compared with $7,076,822 for the Americans. Exports were respectively $6,390,600 and $6,777,000.

Nor could the English in succeeding years catch up with their rivals. In fact their trade began to decrease. In the period from 1820 to 1828 there was a loss of fifteen per cent as compared with their trade of the preceding twenty-five years. The total commerce of the East India Company from 1821 to 1827 as reported to the House of Commons was £16,182,826 and that of the Americans £18,479,698.

This gave the latter an annual average of £382,812 more than the Company. And what proved even more galling to the British was that the American lead was in part due to the fact that American ships were bringing to Canton British manufactured goods at the rate of £200,000 a year.

'The ruinous competition which the Company's Woollen investment has had to contend with, during the last few years, from the introduction of British Manufactures by Americans,' reported the Select Committee of the East India Company at Canton in 1821, 'has been gradually increasing, but its injurious effects have never perhaps been more seriously felt than at present.'

How could the Americans undermine the monopoly of the great and mighty East India Company? The explanation seems largely to lie in the informality of their trade and consequent slight overhead. The Company had its dignity and prestige to maintain; it had traditions which could not be broken. Its great ships were almost all over one thousand tons — the *Earl of Balcarras* built in 1815 was 1417 tons — and carried crews ranging from 107 to 133 men. They were the last word in safety, comfort, and luxury, but had not been built for either speed or efficiency. They simply could not compete with the little American ships which could make two voyages to their one, were sailed by what appeared to the British to be skeleton crews, and carried on their business at Canton with an efficiency and dispatch — sometimes remaining in port for little more than two weeks — which the servants of the Honorable Company could not hope to emulate.

It was no wonder that every interest in England combined in attacking the East India Company when it failed to hold its position against the Americans and yet refused to allow independent English traders to invade its monopoly. Protracted hearings were held in Parliament and countless witnesses, both English and American, were examined. The inevitable result was that the special privileges of the Company were withdrawn, and in 1834 the China trade was thrown open to private merchants who might better be able to compete with the private merchants of the United States. In the clash of commercial rivalries in China, David had slain Goliath.

The most important result of this development upon the American trade was that the importation of British manufactures fell off, due to the new competition of English merchants, and a certain impetus was given to the trade in domestic products. Bills of exchange on London maintained the supremacy which specie had formerly held, but instead of bringing back nankeens the Americans began taking cotton to China, and Lowell sheetings and drillings found a prominent place in ships' manifests. Cotton imports at Canton, which began in 1826 with a value of $15,777, ran as high as $357,332 in 1841.

Otherwise the last two decades of the old China trade show, with few exceptions, that imports at Canton were following familiar lines. If furs became almost a negligible item, there was some ginseng imported, South American copper, lead ingots from Gibraltar, a little steel from England and Sweden, rice from Batavia and Manila, quicksilver, iron, tobacco, candles, beef, Turkish opium, ships' supplies of all sorts, various South Sea products such as *bêche de mer*, mother of pearl, or sharks' fins, and a few American novelties like the watches and music-boxes which Samuel Shaw was first called upon to present to the Canton customs officials.

The most significant change which exports from Canton had undergone was that tea had grown more and more important until it amounted to more than eighty per cent of the entire trade. Not only had nankeens disappeared from home cargoes as the Americans began bringing cotton to China instead of carrying it away, but silk exports had become greatly reduced due to changes in fashions — falling off from $1,317,846 in 1821 to $285,773 in 1841 — and the demand for chinaware had virtually died out because of the introduction in America of French and English porcelain. There was, of course, some trade in such products as cassia, matting, crapes and shawls, sweetmeats, fireworks, lacquer and horn ware, rhubarb, pearl buttons, or Chinese paintings, but it amounted to little.

By 1841 the China trade was the tea trade pure and simple, and American ships were bringing home about fifteen million pounds every year. It was a trade protected by the Government through a system which allowed the withholding of duties for eighteen months, and it gave to China an importance which no one in 1838, when the first sale of Assam tea was recorded, could have believed would come to be shared with India and Ceylon.

If there was little change in most of the ships trading at Canton, it nevertheless is still true that in the very closing years of our period the commerce with the Far East led to the most dramatic and thrilling development which ship-building has ever experienced. The China trade gave birth to the clipper ship.

The first full-rigged ship to be built along the lines of the fast little Baltimore schooners from which the name 'clipper' was derived, according to Arthur H. Clark in 'The Clipper Ship Era,' was the *Ann McKim*, four hundred and ninety-three tons. She was destined for the China trade and for a number of years sailed on the Pacific route. Clark de-

scribes her as a remarkably handsome vessel. Her frames
were of live-oak, copper-fastened throughout, her bottom
sheathed with specially imported red copper, and her fit-
tings of mahogany. She mounted twelve brass guns and
carried three skysail yards and royal studding sails.

But although the *Ann McKim* proved to be unusually
fast, her carrying capacity was small, and consequently no
other ships were constructed along her lines. Then in 1839
the *Akbar*, six hundred and fifty tons, was built for John
M. Forbes. On her first passage to Canton this fine vessel,
constructed somewhat more on clipper ship lines, made the
voyage from New York in one hundred and nine days. The
experiment was so successful that the *Akbar* was quickly
followed by a series of vessels, which, although they still
were not extreme clipper ships, distinctly pointed the way
to that ultimate perfection of shipbuilding.

The *Helena*, six hundred and fifty tons, made several
remarkable passages to China for N. L. and G. Griswold.
The *Paul Jones*, six hundred and twenty tons, owned by
John M. Forbes and Russell and Company, commanded by
Captain Nathaniel B. Palmer, of Antarctic fame, arrived
at Hongkong one hundred and eleven days out of Boston
on her first voyage in 1843, and some years later made the
run from Java Head to New York in seventy-six days. The
*Houqua*, a seven-hundred-and-six-ton ship also commanded
by Captain Palmer, made Java Head seventy-two days out
of New York and Hongkong in another twelve. On the
return voyage she sailed from China to New York in ninety
days. Others among the early clippers were the *Montauk*,
the *Panama*, and the *Coquette*, the last making Canton
from Boston in ninety-nine days. The distance between
Canton and the Atlantic Coast was rapidly shrinking.
Just half the time required at the end of the nineteenth

century was now necessary to sail between the Eastern and Western worlds.

Faster runs were still to be made, however, and when the demands of the China trade resulted in the construction of the *Rainbow*, seven hundred and fifty tons, for the New York firm of Howland and Aspinwall, the extreme clipper ship made its bow to a skeptical and then enthusiastic seafaring world. So sharp were the *Rainbow's* lines that shipping authorities questioned whether she would be able to sail, but when launched in 1845 all doubts were quickly dispelled. On her second voyage to Canton she went out against the monsoon in ninety-two days and was home in eighty-eight. The round trip, including two weeks in port for discharging and loading cargo, took six months and fourteen days — the *Empress of China* on its first voyage had taken fourteen months and nineteen days — and the *Rainbow* brought to her owners the news of her own arrival in Canton.

'Captain John Land, her able and enthusiastic commander,' writes Clark, 'declared that she was the fastest ship in the world, and this was undeniably true; finding no one to differ from him, he further gave it as his opinion that no ship could be built to outsail the *Rainbow*, and it is also true that very few vessels have ever broken her record.'

This brings us to the end of our period, and the further exploits of the clipper ships of the China trade are another story. But the day was clearly foreshadowed when, with the British Navigation Laws repealed and the tea trade concentrated at Shanghai, these fast-sailing American vessels were for a time almost to drive the English vessels from the Eastern seas. The clipper ships could so outsail their rivals that the latter would often be refused cargoes while the Americans invariably loaded as soon as they put into port and were quickly away under their great clouds of canvas in spectacular 16,000-mile races to get the first teas to the London market.

England was then forced to follow America's example and build her own clipper ships, and in 1866 there was a race from Foochow to London among these British vessels which is without parallel in the annals of sailing. It has no concern with the old China trade as far as the United States is concerned, but it is difficult to omit the story in any account which even touches upon China and the clipper ships.

Five vessels sailed from Foochow for London within three days in May, 1866, all loaded with the first teas of the season. The *Fiery Cross* was the first to get away on the morning of the twenty-ninth. The *Ariel* left at ten-thirty, the *Serica* and the *Taeping* at ten-fifty on the thirtieth, and at midnight on the thirty-first sailed the *Taitsing*. Carrying all sail as they jockeyed for the lead in a race in which continents served as the marking buoys, the five vessels passed through the Straits of Sunda, across the Indian Ocean, and about the Cape of Good Hope never more than four or five days apart. Now one and then another stretched out in the lead as it caught a better wind or left its rivals becalmed.

At the Cape of Good Hope it was the *Fiery Cross* which was still in the van with the *Taitsing* trailing the whole fleet. Then coming up on the Azores the *Ariel* jumped to the front, and the *Taitsing* passed the *Taeping*, the *Serica*, and even the *Fiery Cross*. Nearing the entrance to the British Channel the *Taeping* and the *Serica* crept up on the new leaders, passing both the *Taitsing* and the *Fiery Cross*, closing in on the *Ariel*.

At the Lizard the *Taeping* was on the *Ariel's* heels, and the two vessels, ninety days out of Foochow, sighted each other and raced up the Channel side by side. They picked up pilots at the same time, passed Deal eight minutes apart with the *Ariel* in the lead. The *Serica* was four hours behind them, the *Fiery Cross* one day, and the *Taitsing* two. But while the *Ariel* was the first to cross the finish line, its eight-minute lead was cancelled because the *Taeping* had sailed from Foochow twenty minutes later. Victory consequently went to the latter vessel. It had won by twelve minutes on a 16,000-mile course!

Those were thrilling days for men who went to sea. The China trade had served to introduce the first clipper ships; in these races it marked the final summit of their glory.

# CHAPTER IX

## AMERICAN RELATIONS WITH THE CHINESE

In their relations with the Chinese, the Americans at Canton were governed by but one consideration: the promotion of their trade. It was to exchange their specie, their furs, or their cotton goods for teas and silk that they had come to Canton, and everything else was completely subordinated to that one end. Far from the protection of their Government, isolated in the midst of an alien people who continued to regard all foreigners as barbarians, the Americans could have no hope of maintaining any rights to which they might feel themselves entitled as citizens of a sovereign state. They soon realized that they were powerless to uphold any such theory as that of political equality with the Chinese.

The other foreigners were in much the same situation, but the English were until 1834 represented by a powerful trading company which could command the support of the British Government. For the Americans there was no parallel authority. Their little community was made up of small firms and individual merchants in strenuous competition with each other and seldom able to bring any concerted pressure upon the Chinese officials for the protection of American interests. Some half-dozen companies conducted the bulk of the business done in behalf of the merchants at home — such as Russell and Company, D. W. C. Olyphant, Augustine Heard, and W. S. Wetmore — and the permanent American residents at Canton averaged between forty and fifty, but the community had no acknowledged leader. There was no American official comparable to the

President of the Select Committee of the East India Company or to the British Superintendent of Trade.

It is true that there was an American Consul. Samuel Shaw had received the first commission to this post from the hands of Congress itself, and at somewhat irregular intervals the State Department designated various of the merchants resident at Canton as his successors. But these men were never recognized by the Chinese and barely acknowledged by their countrymen. Their duties were to administer the estates of the dead, discipline mutinous sailors, care for the improvident, and report to Washington on the trade. Even for such innocuous tasks they could not count upon the full support of independent and jealous traders. 'The secret manner of transacting business at Canton,' complained Consul Samuel Snow in 1800, 'made it almost impossible to obtain accurate knowledge of the cargoes in the common way.'

The official Chinese attitude toward this nominal representative of the United States Government was first shown in 1799 when permission was sought to fly the American flag before the factory which the early traders had been given for the transaction of their business. The hoppo refused to treat directly with the American Consul, and although the privilege he sought was eventually granted through the medium of the East India Company, the rule was laid down that all favors sought by the Americans must be requested through the hong merchants and none but verbal communications would be exchanged with the Consul.

At the time when the British were impressing American seamen with complete disregard of the rights of both the United States and of China, the impotence of the Consul became especially conspicuous. He had no way of making those official protests which in another country would have been received as a direct complaint of the United States Government. All that the Americans could do was to address a memorial to the 'Governor of the Province of Canton,' vainly attempting to remind him of his international obligations.

In view of later developments and the subsequent conflict between Chinese and Americans over legal jurisdiction within China, this memorial is of significant interest as showing the American attitude of that day. There was then no questioning of China's absolute sovereignty. This first expression of opinion on a problem which later led to the demand for extraterritoriality declared:

That by the ancient and well established laws and usages of all civilized nations, the persons and property of friendly foreigners within the territory and jurisdiction of a sovereign and independent Empire, are under the special protection of the government thereof, and any violence or indignity offered to such persons or to the flag of the nation to which they belong, is justly considered as done to the government within whose territory the outrage is committed;

That by the same law of nations, the civil and military agents of the government are strictly prohibited from assuming any authority whatever within the territory of the other nor can they seize the person of the highest state criminal, who may have eluded the justice of their own!

There was no result to this memorial, however, and aroused by this new evidence of the futility of a consul who had no access to Chinese officialdom and no way of upholding American interests, the resident merchants in Canton memorialized President Jefferson. Some indication of official support was sought for the Consul, some tangible evidence which might be shown to the Chinese as proving that when he spoke, he spoke with the authority of the United States Government.

Nothing was done. Washington remained supremely indifferent to the conditions under which Americans lived and traded at Canton. With the one gesture of appointing a consul, the Government officially divorced the American merchants in China and left them completely to their own devices.[1] If they hoped to develop their trade, there consequently was no policy open to them but one of complete acquiescence to every restriction which the Chinese saw fit to impose. This was an attitude which contrasted strongly with the vigor and daring with which they had developed their commerce in the Far East, but friendship had to be maintained at all costs. Even if it served to strengthen Canton's arrogant mandarins in their conviction that the barbarians within their borders could be ruled exactly as they saw fit, no other way was open.

Samuel Shaw had had a first experience of where such a policy might lead and had vainly fought against it in a case which really concerned the English. But his attempt to inspire the foreigners to stand together in defense of their rights had failed, and the necessity of surrender where there was no chance of victory was not lost upon his successors.

Soon after Shaw had arrived in Canton on his first voyage, a Chinese had been accidentally killed by a salute from a British vessel, the *Lady Hughes*. The Canton authorities demanded that the gunner be given up, as they declared that Chinese law called for a life for a life, but the English refused to deliver their countryman to the tender mercies of Chinese justice. Whereupon the Chinese seized the supercargo of the offending vessel, ordered that all trade with the foreigners be suspended, and withdrew from the foreign settlement all the Chinese servants.

[1] For a period of fifty years a regularly appointed consul was resident in Canton only fourteen. He was invariably without instructions.

The situation was critical. The boat crews of the vessels at Whampoa, including that of the *Empress of China*, were brought up-river to defend the factories, if necessary by force, while on the river opposite the settlement the Chinese massed forty of their warships.

Shaw now took the lead in urging a united front on the part of all concerned to force the Chinese to surrender their hostage and reach a peaceful solution of the controversy. But there was no feeling of unity among these rival traders. The French, the Danes, and the Dutch frankly refused to risk hostilities on behalf of the English. At a conference with the Canton officials they agreed to send their armed boats back to Whampoa under the Chinese flag in return for permission to carry on their trade, and furthermore promised to exert all their influence upon the English to induce them to give up the gunner of the *Lady Hughes*.

Shaw indignantly refused to desert the British. 'I considered the rights of humanity,' he wrote, 'deeply interested in the present business, to support which I had, at the request of the English chief, ordered the American boat to Canton; that when the English chief assured me that the purposes for which she had been required were answered, I would send her back, and not till then.'

Abandoned by all but the Americans and with their whole trade in jeopardy, the English, however, decided upon surrender. They gave up the gunner, despite his complete innocence of anything remotely resembling premeditated murder, to the pleasant fate of strangulation. Peace and commerce were thereupon restored.

'Thus ended a very troublesome affair,' wrote the forthright American who had initiated our commerce with China, 'which commenced in confusion, was carried on without order, and terminated disgracefully. Had that spirit of union among the Europeans taken place which the rights of humanity demanded, and could private interest have been for a moment sacrificed to the general good, the conclusion of the matter must have been honorable, and probably some additional privilege would have been obtained. But as it did terminate, we can only apply to it the observation of the Chinese themselves — "Truly, all Fanquois have much lose his face in this business."'

The power of stopping trade through which the Chinese had brought the English to terms in this controversy became a weapon against which the foreigners could develop no protection. The Americans had learned their lesson, and so made the most of what privileges were granted them, accepting the circumscribed life of Canton as cheerfully as they could. It was not as impossible a situation as it might appear to be to-day. For while the mandarin officials were proud and scornful, convinced that 'if the foreigners are deprived of the tea and rhubarb of China for several days, they are afflicted with blindness and constipation of the bowels, to that degree that their lives are in the greatest danger,' the hong merchants were neither so ignorant nor so conceited.[1] Consequently their attitude was uniformly friendly and cordial.

One of the hong merchants who especially smoothed the path of the Americans was the famous merchant Houqua. This Chinese was a shrewd and successful trader whose operations became world-wide in their scope and whose teas

[1] This idea of the foreigners' dependence on tea and rhubarb was generally prevalent in China. A much later report on foreign trade declared: 'The foreigners from the West are naturally fond of milk and cream; indulgence in these luxuries induces costiveness, when there is nothing but rhubarb and tea which will clear their system and restore their spirits; if once deprived of these articles they are immediately laid up with sickness.... If we cut off the trade of the barbarians, turbulence and disorder will ensue in their own countries; and this is the first reason why they must have our goods.'

HOUQUA, CHINESE MERCHANT

were shipped to all parts of the world, not only by the
American merchants, but on his own account. His word
was as good as his bond and his *chop* on a chest of tea, in
London or Amsterdam as well as in New York or Philadelphia, a certain guarantee of its excellence. He had his
own contacts with the great English bankers, Baring
Brothers, through whom the Americans financed so much
of their trade, and prided himself on the international
character of his business connections. He even invested in
American securities.

His wealth was fantastic. While several other hong merchants had failed or been forced into bankruptcy, his fortune had steadily mounted. The authorities knew this, knew
it only too well, and he was forced to make enormous contri-
butions to their periodic levies upon the Canton trade. At
one time he had to pay $1,000,000 to make up the debts
of certain of his brother merchants and at another $1,100,-
000 for the ransom of Canton. Yet his wealth was estimated
in 1834 at $26,000,000, probably the largest mercantile for-
tune in the world at that time.

Houqua was always particularly cordial toward newcomers, and his friendship for John P. Cushing, the most
successful of all the merchants at Canton, who retired with
a fortune comparable to that of Houqua himself, was ad-
mittedly the greatest factor in the outstanding position
Cushing came to hold in the community. But the most
remarkable example of his generosity was that shown to a
Boston merchant who had failed.

This man, as we are told by William C. Hunter, was
anxious to wind up his affairs as best he could and return to
America. Houqua held his promissory note for $72,000 and
the Bostonian had no way of meeting this obligation. One
day Houqua asked him to call. 'You and I are No. 1 "olo

flen,"' Houqua is reputed to have said to his debtor; 'you belong honest man, only no got chance.' Then taking out the promissory note the Chinese merchant calmly tore it up and threw it into the waste-basket, casually remarking, 'Just now have settee counter, alla finishee; you go, you please.'

The story may or may not be apocryphal, but it has long been taken as symbolic of the pleasant relations between the Chinese and American merchants when there was no interference from Manchu officialdom. Their interests were so nearly identical, moreover, that they were at one in trying to smooth over every incident which might mean a clash with authority. For if the Americans had no effective way of upholding their rights in conflict with the officials, the hong merchants were even more under their control. The Government appointed the members of the co-hong and held them responsible for everything concerned with the foreign trade.

The success with which the Americans and Chinese co-operated along these lines is attested by William C. Hunter. 'Everything worked smoothly and harmoniously,' he wrote in his memoirs of the life of old Canton, 'by acting in direct opposition to what we were ordered to do.... We pursued the evil tenor of our ways with supreme indifference, took care of our business, pulled boats, walked, dined well, and so the years rolled by as happily as possible.'

Unfortunately there were times when the foreign community could not escape official interference. It was impossible for relations with the Chinese populace always to run a smooth course.

American sailors visiting the grogshops of Hog Lane could not invariably be counted upon to conduct themselves with decorum, especially when the chief aim of the Chinese shop-

keepers was to get them drunk and then fleece them un-
mercifully. A British witness once testified before the
House of Lords that the Americans were 'far more orderly
and better conducted than the British seamen,' but nevertheless sanguinary clashes with the Cantonese were not
always avoided.

The rabble of Canton were in fact often encouraged by
the officials to express their scorn and derision of the
'foreign devils' as boisterously as they pleased. When
the residents of the foreign settlement attempted to make
any excursions about the neighboring countryside, they
often found themselves forced to beat a hurried retreat to
the factories in the face of a barrage of insulting epithets
and small stones. In one instance Henry Trowbridge, who
had sailed on the *Betsy's* sealing voyage in 1801, found
himself mobbed at the city gates and only escaped by
scattering handfuls of small coins, which diverted the attention of the Chinese long enough to let him get away.

Under these conditions the wonder is not that there were
a number of riots and consequent deaths among Chinese or
foreigners, but that there were not far more. In the event of
the latter being killed, it is to the credit of the Chinese that
they invariably took prompt action against the guilty.
One such case was that of the ship *Wabash*, of Baltimore,
which lost four of its crew through a pirate attack. The
Canton authorities promptly captured thirteen of the
pirates and executed five of them. 'To be murdered by
pirates,' the Viceroy declared in making recompense for the
lives lost, 'is an extremely lamentable case.' This was a
satisfying exhibition of Chinese justice; the trouble arose
when a Chinese had been killed.

According to Chinese law a willful murder was punished
by beheading; killing in an affray, even though accidentally,

carried the penalty of death by strangulation;[1] and a purely accidental death without intent even to injure could be compensated by payment of a fine. These laws were clear and well defined. But they were not applied to foreigners as they were to Chinese. The principle on which the Canton authorities acted was that contained in an imperial edict of 1749, which bluntly demanded, in order to restrain those 'beyond the pale of civilization,' a life for a life in every case in which a Chinese met death at the hands of a foreigner.

Behind this theory there was also the Chinese idea of group responsibility, which was entirely foreign to the principles of European or American jurisprudence. If an American killed a Chinese, no matter what the circumstances, the American community was held responsible. An American had to be delivered up to satisfy the demand of a life for a life, and it mattered not at all to the Chinese whether or not the individual surrendered was really guilty. Justice would be satisfied by his execution.

It has already been noted how this principle worked out in practice in the case of the unfortunate gunner of the *Lady Hughes*, and in succeeding years the English were involved in a number of similar cases. On one occasion they succeeded in persuading the Chinese to accept the death of one man who had really been killed in a drunken affray as an accidental homicide. In another the death of a Cantonese was shortly followed by the suicide of a butcher on an English ship, and the Chinese authorities complacently reported to Peking that it was this man who had been the murderer. Not until 1821, when a Chinese woman was reported to have been killed by a sailor on the Balti-

---

[1] Strangulation was a lesser penalty than beheading because the body was not disfigured.

more ship *Emily*, Captain Cowpland, did the Americans find themselves in the position of having to declare whether or not they were prepared to accept Chinese justice.

The circumstances of the death of this woman were obscure. The Chinese claimed that she had been struck by a jar hurled by a sailor named Francis Terranova. Captain Cowpland denied that she had been wounded by any one on his ship and declared that she had simply fallen from the small boat in which she was peddling fruit for the American sailors and had been drowned. His case was weakened, however, because Consul Wilcocks made an attempt to bribe the woman's family to agree that the death was accidental. The Chinese consequently demanded the surrender of Terranova, citing the *Wabash* case as justification of their right to do so.

The American residents at Canton thereupon held a meeting to decide what course of action they should follow. It resulted in a definite alignment of the sea captains on one side and the merchants and supercargoes on the other. Captain Cowpland absolutely refused to surrender his seaman, and with the backing of his brother officers declared he was ready to defend his ship by force against any Chinese attempt to seize the alleged culprit. It was the attitude to be expected of the seamen of the China trade. But the merchants and supercargoes, men whose primary interest, or rather sole interest, was their trade, were just as strongly opposed to force and favored the surrender of Terranova to prevent any interruption to their commerce. In their behalf it may be said that there was a strong presumption of the sailor's guilt, but nevertheless what they sought was peace at any price.

To settle this issue a committee was appointed of five captains, five supercargoes, and five resident merchants.

Their decision, a tempered victory for the traders as opposed to the seamen, was to adopt a policy of non-resistance. Terranova was not to be surrendered, but the Chinese might try him for murder aboard the *Emily*. To this programme the Canton officials agreed.

The trial was duly held, but it was an absolute farce. The mandarin charged with the investigation came aboard the *Emily* convinced of the guilt of the accused and determined to convict him as speedily as possible. He refused to hear evidence, refused to allow the charges to be translated into English, and finally broke off the trial, abruptly declaring Terranova guilty and demanding his immediate surrender.

This the Americans first refused, but when the Chinese backed up their demands by stopping trade, a compromise was agreed upon. Terranova still would not be given up, but if the authorities attempted to seize him by force no resistance would be offered, on condition that he was given another trial at Canton. This condition was but a salve to the American conscience. The fate of Terranova now became certain and there was no reason for surprise when he was seized a few days later, given a second even more farcical trial to which no Americans were admitted, and then summarily strangled.

In announcing their policy on the Terranova case the Americans at Canton made a statement which completely clarifies their position on the question of Chinese jurisdiction. It clearly shows that since they could hope for no backing from their own government, there had been no change in those ideas which they first expressed in their complaints to the Chinese Government on British interference with their shipping.

'We are bound to submit to your laws while we are in your waters,' they told the Chinese, 'be they ever so unjust. We will not resist them. You have, following upon your ideas of justice, condemned the man unheard. But the flag of our country has never been disgraced. It now waves over you. It is no disgrace to submit to your power, surrounded as we are by an overwhelming force, backed by that of a great empire. You have the power to compel us. We believe the man innocent, when he is taken from the ship we leave her; and the commander strikes his colors.'

A rather equivocal statement. Hardly the words of men prepared to defend at all costs the cause of justice. The merchants and supercargoes had clearly enough outvoted the captains. Principle had been abandoned for the sake of trade. But the significance of the Terranova case does not lie so much in this forced acceptance of Chinese justice. In reality it planted the seeds of extraterritoriality. It showed the need of some guarantee behind which stood the United States Government whereby Americans would never again be compelled to make such an abject surrender of their ideas of justice.

To the English, who were struggling for the right to administer their own criminal laws in China, no words were too harsh for what they regarded as the betrayal of a common cause. The case of the *Lady Hughes*, when it was Samuel Shaw who had stood out for resistance to the Chinese demands for the surrender of the innocent gunner, and the English who had sacrificed him for the sake of their trade, was completely forgotten. The 'unaccountable apathy and total absence of exertion' which seemed in British eyes to mark the case were bitterly assailed on all sides. The Select Committee of the East India Company reported to London that the Americans 'had barbarously abandoned a man serving under their Flag to the sanguinary laws of this Empire without an endeavor to obtain common justice for him.' It declared that their conduct 'deserves to be held in eternal execration by every Moral, honorable and feeling Mind.'

But what could the Americans have done? They were realists. Their Government was beyond reach and in any event could not have been expected to take any action whatsoever in their support. To have held Terranova by force would have meant the entire stoppage of their trade and probably forced their withdrawal from Canton. The thought of how advantageous this might have been to the East India Company may have colored British opinion.

A full report on the Terranova case was sent to Washington by Consul Wilcocks but no official comment was ever made upon it. Canton was still too far away.

Only in one respect was there evidence that the Government felt any responsibility at all toward the American trade with China from the time of the *Empress of China's* first voyage to the close of our period. Occasional visits were made to Far Eastern waters by vessels of war.

The first of these was that of the frigate *Congress*. In 1800 it had been sent out against French privateers and cruised as far as the Straits of Sunda but in 1819 it was dispatched for the specific purpose of offering some protection to American ships against Chinese pirates. Under the command of Captain John Dandridge Henley, a nephew of Martha Washington, it anchored off the island of Lintin. All foreign war vessels were forbidden to remain in Chinese waters but the English had disregarded this rule on the pretence of obtaining supplies and the American commander was ready to follow their example, much to the perturbation of the Chinese. Finally the officials agreed to allow the *Congress* to re-provision — 'a piece of kindness beyond the limits of strict propriety' — but at the same time they issued an edict that the foreign vessel would not be allowed 'to make further pretexts to gain time and linger about.'

It is an interesting example of the American policy of acquiescence in all Chinese regulations that the residents at Canton viewed the presence of the *Congress* with some embarrassment. For fear of offending the authorities they refused Captain Henley's offer to convoy their ships and it was with great relief that they saw him leave Chinese waters without any untoward incident to trouble the peaceful atmosphere of Canton.

The next of such visitors was the *Vincennes*, Captain William B. Finch, which in 1830 was the first American war vessel to circumnavigate the globe. By this time it was felt that visits by war vessels might possibly have some effect upon the position of the Americans in China through the evidence they offered of the naval power of the United States, but nevertheless the *Vincennes's* commander was cautioned against any infringement of Chinese customs. Only if a careful course was pursued, the Canton residents told Captain Finch, could it be hoped that these visits would be of benefit in allaying the 'petty delays and impositions peculiar to our flag.'

The frigate *Potomac* and the sloop-of-war *Peacock* were among other such vessels to anchor in Chinese waters. The latter had as a passenger Edmund Roberts, who was on a mission which was to result in the first treaties of the United States with Eastern powers, those with Muscat and Siam, but the Chinese had no idea of according him any diplomatic privileges. Their order to the American war vessels was that they should 'unfurl their sails and return home; they will not be permitted to delay and loiter about, and the day of their departure must be made known. Hasten, hasten!'

It is only too apparent that throughout this period nothing was further from the thoughts of either the Chinese or the Americans in Canton than any idea of present or future political relations between their two countries. What American policy toward China there was remained simply the policy of the Americans actually in China. Their Government had no concern in it and it was dictated purely and simply by the demands of trade as interpreted by the merchants at Canton.

Inevitably under these conditions that policy was conciliatory and pacific. Even in such a crisis as the Terranova case the Americans had to surrender. Far more than the English, with the power of the East India Company behind them, they had to submit with the best grace possible to whatever the Canton officials demanded. One happy result of their attitude was that they won the confidence of the Chinese and almost unconsciously a basis for Sino-American friendship was established which still endures.

# CHAPTER X

## OPIUM AND EQUALITY

WHILE relations between the Americans and the Chinese were on the whole satisfactory enough to reconcile the former to the conditions of their life at Canton, this was not altogether true in the case of the English. They resented far more than did the merchants of Boston and New York the restrictions on their trade, and because of their position in other countries of the East, felt more keenly China's cool assumption of superiority. Furthermore, a question on which we have not yet touched, that of the trade in opium, was slowly coming to a head. It was to prove, as an editorial in the 'Chinese Repository' stated, the 'great proximate cause' of the first Anglo-Chinese war.

England traded with China under conditions exactly paralleling those of the American trade. It had, however, in 1793 and again in 1816, sought to win from the Chinese an extension of its privileges and some form of political recognition.

The first British embassy to China was sent out under Lord Macartney and had proceeded to Peking amid much pomp and circumstance. There was only one disturbing note in the impressive spectacle of the ambassador making his ceremonious way to the court of the Son of Heaven. The barges and carts which carried to the Emperor Ch'ien Lung the presents of George the Third bore streaming pennants with the inscription, 'Ambassador bearing tribute from the country of England.' It was a slight to British dignity of which Lord Macartney was compelled to pretend ignorance, for a protest would have meant the end of his embassy.

At Jehol, a city just beyond the Great Wall where the English were forced to follow the Emperor to his country seat, the ambassador was met with the demand that he comply with the ceremony of the kowtow. This Lord Macartney refused to do unless a Chinese official of equal rank performed a similar obeisance before a picture of George the Third. The tribute-bearing flags had been enough. The ambassador could not afford any further sacrifice of the dignity and prestige of his country through an act which in the minds of the Chinese would have been regarded as a full acknowledgment of British vassalage.

Finally the Emperor consented to receive him if he paid the same homage before the imperial throne as he was accustomed to pay before that of his own sovereign, and with this question settled, the interview which Lord Macartney had come so far to seek at last took place. But with that inconsequential triumph to his credit, the work of Lord Macartney came to an end. Despite the cordiality of the Chinese, it was soon evident that not only would the Emperor refuse to consider any such thing as a treaty with Great Britain, but that he had no intention of concerning himself in any way with the relations between the two countries or with the trade at Canton. The latter was far beneath his notice.

When the Emperor returned to Peking, the British mission followed him, but it was soon politely hinted that it might as well continue on its journey to the coast and return to England. Lord Macartney was reluctantly forced to abandon all hope of accomplishing anything. He returned overland to Canton, again conducted with pomp and circumstance, but with empty hands.

'Never was an embassy deserving of better success,' wrote the French missionary Grammont, 'whether it be

considered on account of the experience, wisdom, and
amiable qualities of Lord Macartney and Sir George
Staunton; or of the talents, the knowledge, and the circum-
spect behaviour of the gentlemen who composed their suite;
or of the valuable and curious presents intended for the
Emperor — and yet, strange to tell, never was an embassy
that succeeded so ill!'

One important thing it accomplished, however. Through
the fascinating journals kept by members of the party,
especially that of Sir George Staunton — 'An Authentic
Account of an Embassy from the King of Great Britain
to the Emperor of China' — a new understanding of China,
its civilization, and its attitude toward the West was spread
throughout both England and the United States. Staunton's book was brought out in America in 1799, while the
curious account of the embassy by Æneas Anderson, Lord
Macartney's valet, had an American edition as early as
1795.

The next attempt of the English to reach some understanding with China was inspired by the friction over the
activities of H.M.S. *Doris*, general impatience with the restrictions in force at Canton, and a desire to assure Peking
that England had no hostile intentions toward China.
Lord Amherst headed this embassy and his experiences
were even more discouraging than had been those of Lord
Macartney. The journey to Peking was marked by eternal
haggling over the kowtow. Lord Amherst refused to consider it, and consequently he was told upon his arrival at
the capital that the Emperor Chia Ch'ing, who had succeeded Ch'ien Lung, would not receive him and that the
embassy might as well turn back. So after a fruitless journey of sixteen thousand miles the ambassador left Peking
without even a sight of the imperious ruler who permitted

no other king or emperor in the world to address him on terms of equality.

At Canton commerce proceeded as best it could despite these rebuffs, and it was not until 1834, when the monopoly of the East India Company was abolished, that any further attempt was made to establish any sort of political relationship between England and China. In that year Lord Napier was sent out to Canton as Chief Superintendent of Trade to represent those British interests which had formerly been protected by the President of the East India Company's Select Committee.

The unfortunate controversy and personal tragedy which were the result of this move were due to a mixture of pride and ignorance on the part of both the Superintendent of Trade and the Viceroy at Canton. The instructions laid down by Palmerston to guide Lord Napier's policy had been on the whole highly conciliatory, but they included one brief sentence: 'Your lordship will announce your arrival at Canton by letter to the Viceroy.' This was completely at variance with the Chinese rule that all official communications should be made through the hong merchants and that they should be petitions, not letters, while it also gave to Lord Napier an official status which the Viceroy was not prepared to acknowledge. Consequently, he refused to accept Lord Napier's letter when it was presented to his officers and sent orders to Macao, where the British official had stopped, that he would not be allowed to come to Canton until the Emperor had been memorialized.

In a communication to the hong merchants expostulating on the effrontery of the British in sending him a letter in which 'there was absurdly written the character *Great English Nation*,' the Viceroy was carried away by his outraged feelings. 'To sum up the whole matter, the nation has its laws,' he exclaimed. 'Even England has its laws. How much more the Celestial Empire! How flaming bright are its great laws and ordinances! More terrible than the awful thunderbolts! Under this whole bright heaven, none dares to disobey them.'

That is, except the British official. For Lord Napier had already left for Canton without waiting to secure permission. Whereupon after a futile conference in which some minor Chinese officials condescended to meet the British Superintendent, a conference known as the 'Battle of the Chairs,' for it largely resolved itself into a contest over precedence, all British trade was stopped and the Viceroy issued a proclamation savagely attacking Lord Napier's 'stupidity and obstinacy.' The Chinese servants were withdrawn from the British factory, the people of Canton were ordered on pain of death not to sell provisions to the British, and the other foreigners were warned not to offer them any assistance if they did not wish to call down upon themselves the same penalties.

Lord Napier's answer was to order the British frigates *Imogene* and *Andromache*, then at Macao, to force the passage of the Bogue. They made their way under fire to Whampoa and sent a guard of marines on to the British factory. In an open manifesto the Superintendent of Trade combated all the charges which the Chinese had made against him and charged the Viceroy with opening the preliminaries of war.

A counter-proclamation was promptly issued. The Viceroy declared that although a 'headman' had been substituted for a 'taipan,' the English were still obligated to communicate with the Canton authorities through the hong merchants, that no official intimation of Lord Napier's coming had been received, that the Superintendent of

Trade had broken the laws of the Empire by bringing armed forces to the foreign settlement, and finally warned the English that he could easily overwhelm them with the thousands of troops at his disposal.

'Considering that the said nation's King has hitherto been in the highest degree reverently obedient,' the manifesto declared, 'he cannot in sending Lord Napier at this time have desired him thus obstinately to resist.' The question of trade was disposed of with typical Chinese arrogance. Characterizing tea and rhubarb in the familiar fashion as 'sources by which the said nation's people live and maintain life,' the Viceroy said China's imports from abroad were unimportant and the duties on the British trade 'concern not the Celestial Empire the extent of a hair or a feather's down.'

The situation was now more critical than it had been at any time in the course of British trade with China, and neither side showed any signs of surrendering. But on September 14, after he had been in Canton less than two months, Lord Napier gave in. He was seriously ill and also convinced that his quarrel with the Viceroy should not be allowed to ruin the season's trade, so he left Canton with a convoy of eight armed boats and returned to Macao. During the trip down-river, he was subjected to so many delays and annoyances by the Chinese authorities that his illness was greatly aggravated. His return to Macao meant for the English merchants the removal of the embargo on their trade; for Lord Napier it resulted in his death.

In this incident the English had a legitimate excuse for forcing to an issue a question which it was perhaps inevitable should some day have to be settled by either force or the threat of force. Lord Napier had blundered in offending against Chinese prejudices, and in seeking political recognition had attempted something for which he had no real warrant from the Chinese point of view. Nevertheless, the Canton authorities had deliberately affronted the political power of Great Britain. Ignorant as they might be of international law and of the customs of the West, they unquestionably knew just what they were doing. In addition, their treatment of Lord Napier undoubtedly hastened his death.

Throughout his stay in Canton the British official had continually urged Palmerston to give him the backing which might enable him to win his case against the Chinese. 'I can only once more implore your lordship,' he wrote in one of his dispatches, 'to force them to acknowledge my authority and the King's commission.' The British merchants also besought their Government to make at least that show of force which they were convinced would effectively persuade China to accept political relations and open up the trade more widely. But the Government chose to take no action whatsoever. It was to wait until a far more ignoble cause goaded it into war.

This was of course opium, and the history of British trade in this pernicious drug goes back as far as 1767 when about a thousand chests were first imported from Bengal by a Chinese merchant. It was used then solely as medicine and entered under this heading in the Chinese tariff. So slight was the demand for it that when the East India Company, thirteen years later, made its first official entrance into the trade with a shipment of twenty-eight hundred chests on behalf of the Bengal Government, the market was overstocked and the opium could not be sold. Nevertheless, the Chinese were quick to see its possible effect upon the populace if its use became general, and as early as 1800 an imperial edict forbade any further importation of the 'vile dirt.'

It continued to be brought to Canton in increasing quantities, however, and even when the original edict was strengthened in 1809 by requiring the hong merchants to give a bond not to import it, vessels loaded with opium continued to anchor at Whampoa with impunity. At last, in 1821, stricter enforcement of the laws drove the opium ships out of the Pearl River, but, far from stopping the trade, this development simply changed the tactics of the traders. There grew up off the island of Lintin, at the mouth of the Pearl River, a floating dépôt, where the opium ships anchored without molestation and transferred their precious cargoes to store ships which in turn sold the drug to Chinese traders.

From now on the trade increased by leaps and bounds. The importation of a thousand chests had swollen to more than nine thousand by the season of 1826–27, and in another ten years it was thirty-four thousand. In 1834–35, a year when the value of the opium imports was placed at $11,758,-779, it was reported that there were thirty-five ships anchored at Lintin and their trade was greater than the legitimate trade at Whampoa. Opium was slowly but surely becoming the most important phase of British commerce with China.

In its official capacity the East India Company had abandoned the carrying trade as early as 1800, and it was the 'country ships,' operating under the Company's license, which brought the drug in its behalf to Canton. But in India the sale of the drug was a Government monopoly, representing an annual income of from one to two million pounds sterling, or some ten per cent of Bengal's total revenues. Moreover, every chest imported in China by the

A CHINESE OPIUM DEN

country ships, according to R. B. Forbes, had a certificate of the East India Company.

The opium trade provided for British commerce a product which always commanded a market at Canton. While the Americans were searching the seas for anything which might be carried to Canton in place of specie, the English could always fall back upon this drug. Not only did it provide a medium of exchange for tea, but it allowed them to export from Canton the silver which the Americans brought there. With their complete monopoly of all the opium grown in India, their commerce naturally had a tremendous advantage over that of the United States.

This does not mean that the Americans either held aloof from the opium trade or were not concerned in it. They did what they could to compete with the British monopoly and moral compunctions governed their attitude no more than they did that of the English traders. This question concerned almost no one except the Chinese. The merchants of the United States imported what they could, but because the sources open to their exploitation were so limited, the opium trade never became for them the vital question which it became for the English.

Smyrna was the source for what little opium the Americans brought to China. Their first venture was some one hundred and twenty-four cases and fifty-one boxes imported in 1805, and two years later the Select Committee of the East India Company was as usual complaining about the new competition and reminding London that if it were not checked, it might seriously injure British trade. But it never grew to large proportions. Statistics are incomplete and conflicting, but the Americans' average importation does not seem to have amounted to more than about five per cent of their total imports, as compared with British importation of thirty-four per cent of their total. In the period from 1818 to 1833, for example, British opium imports were valued at $104,302,948, an average of $6,518,-934, while the American total was reported to have been $4,925,997, or an average of $307,875. The East India Company itself declared that the American share in the opium trade was little more than three per cent.[1]

Almost all the merchants at Canton were concerned in it to a greater or less degree — the Perkinses, the Peabodys, the Russells, the Lows, and the Forbeses — but one firm held carefully aloof. That was Olyphant and Company, whose moral attitude upon opium and friendliness toward missionaries won for the company's factory the name of 'Zion's Corner.'

It was unfortunate that this firm alone looked on the opium question from any other than a purely commercial point of view. For from 1821, when the opium ships first began the practice of anchoring at Lintin, to the crisis of 1839, this inglorious trade became an increasingly serious point of friction between foreigners and Chinese. It was strictly forbidden by Chinese law, but with the connivance of the Chinese officials it could be carried on openly. It gave rise to a system of bribery and corruption almost without parallel, though one cannot escape the feeling that Prohibition in the United States has created conditions in this country somewhat reminiscent of those in China almost a century ago. With the important difference, however, that the chief offenders against the Chinese laws were foreigners.

The opium trade in the second and third decades of the nineteenth century was, in fact, more easily handled than the legitimate trade. It was subject to no taxation except

[1] These statistics are taken from English sources — the reports of the East India Company and Parliamentary Papers.

the charges of unscrupulous officials, and as the opium was always paid for in advance, it promised a definite and high profit. Referring to the happy lot of the opium importer until 1839, William C. Hunter wrote: 'His sales were pleasantness and his remittances were peace. Transactions seemed to partake of the nature of the drug; they imparted a soothing frame of mind with three per cent commission on sales, one per cent on returns, and no bad debts!'

Imperial edicts against the trade were issued again and again, and occasionally a flurry would be caused by the appointment of some new official at Canton who would make an attempt to break up the smuggling, but the sole effect of such measures would be a temporary rise in prices. The mandarins were more likely to make a bluff of driving the ships away than actually to intervene in a business which meant illegal profits for them as well as for the trader. One favorite device was to make a vigorous foray upon Lintin just as the opium ships were sailing for India, and then complacently report to the higher authorities that the foreign vessels had been forced to flee the coast and that the whole trade had been abandoned.

One Chinese admiral had an even more efficient scheme. He made an arrangement with the foreign traders to handle their opium himself. After disposing of the bulk of it at a tremendous profit, he would then hand over a small share to his superiors with the proud boast that he had captured it after a fierce struggle with the smugglers. 'For these eminent services,' wrote the Chinese historian from whom the story is taken, 'he received a peacock's feather and was made a rear-admiral; in consequence of which the yearly imports gradually reached a figure of forty or fifty thousand chests.'

Opium was also sold along the coast. No foreign vessel

was allowed to trade at any Chinese port other than Canton, but there was no reason why the smuggling at Lintin could not also be practiced farther north. Both British and American ships made this experiment and made it successfully. A fleet of fast and well-armed clipper schooners — the *Sylph*, the *Angola*, the *Zephyr*, the *Mazeppa*, and the *Ariel* — was specially built for this traffic. They were able to deliver chests of the forbidden drug with perfect impunity to consignees along the coast, specially designated by the Canton dealers, who had already paid in advance for the opium clipper's whole cargo.

Again it is William C. Hunter, of the firm of Russell and Company, who gives an illuminating story of the foreigners' relations with the Chinese authorities at the forbidden ports.

In 1837 he sailed as a passenger on the clipper schooner *Rose*, which carried a cargo of three hundred chests of the contraband drug, valued at three hundred thousand dollars. Its first stop was at the island of Namoa, near the border between the provinces of Kwangtung and Fukien. No sooner had the *Rose* anchored than it was visited by a Chinese commodore, who dutifully showed to the captain a copy of the imperial edict which declared that a foreign vessel could anchor in the harbor only for necessary supplies and, having received them, 'must no longer loiter, but depart at once.'

This was a formality. Once it had been complied with, the obliging official entered the *Rose's* cabin and with no further beating about the bush asked how much opium the schooner carried. Being told, the question then arose as to 'cumsha,' and it was quickly settled, Hunter writes, on the 'good old Chinese principle of "all same custom."'

His Excellency then consented to drink a glass of wine

and smoke a cheroot. Thereafter he was escorted to the vessel's side and took his place in his gig, where he 'sat majestically in an armchair smoking quietly.' A large embroidered silk umbrella was held over his head and his servants, dressed in grass cloth with conical rattan hats bound with flowing red silk cord, fanned away the flies and mosquitoes while he was rowed back to his junk.

Not another Chinese vessel dared approach the *Rose* until the Commodore had completed his visit, but then the barges of the Chinese opium-buyers immediately surrounded the schooner. The opium, already sold at Canton for delivery at Namao, was handed over and a transaction involving $150,000 completed with no further formalities.

So generally was this nefarious traffic — for it can be justified neither by law nor ethics — condoned throughout this period that even the famous German missionary, the Reverend Charles Gutzlaff, had consented in 1832 to act as an interpreter on a voyage made by the *Sylph*. He wrote that he undertook this strange mission only after 'a conflict in my own mind,' but the point was that it gave him an exceptional opportunity to distribute tracts along the coast. A few years later the brig *Huron* made a northward voyage, in the course of which twenty thousand volumes of Christian propaganda were given away. It is not altogether surprising that Peking should object to this strange union of opium and religion.

It was about 1836 that the opium question really began to arouse the Chinese. Then a veritable deluge of memorials descended upon Peking, penned by anxious officials advising the Son of Heaven how he should deal with the problem. The first of these, written by Hsü Nai-tsi, vice-president of the sacrificial court, urged the Emperor to legalize the traffic on economic grounds. As a contraband trade it caused a tremendous drain in specie, but, he argued, if it was within the law an exchange of opium for goods might be enforced. But this suggestion was quickly answered by memorialists who pointed out that opium was debauching the people and corrupting the officials, and that it was because of its enfeebling effect on the Chinese that the English were importing it. They strenuously urged that the most drastic steps be taken to prevent all smuggling and that both Chinese and foreigners at Canton be warned that unless they complied with the laws all trade would be stopped and the merchants resident at Canton condemned to death.

For a time, while this controversy was raging among the Chinese, the English professed to believe that the opium trade might after all be legalized. But there was little justification for them so much to make the wish father to the thought. One memorial no more meant legalization than one swallow means summer. They were really shutting their eyes to the obvious. The opium question was coming to a crisis.

Only two years after Hsü Nai-tsi's memorial, when there were some thirty opium shops at Lintin and twenty more along the coast, with their sales totaling twenty million dollars, the Chinese gave the foreigners their first taste of how they intended to deal with smugglers. In the square in front of the foreign factories, almost at the foot of the American flagpole, the Canton officials set up the apparatus for the execution of a Chinese trader who had been convicted of dealing in the forbidden drug and prepared in full view of the foreigners for his strangulation.

In immediate and bitter resentment of what they considered an affront aimed directly at them — as it undoubtedly was — a number of English and Americans thereupon attacked the execution officials. After a strenuous mêlée, of which the condemned Chinese was an interested but passive spectator, the officials were forced to withdraw from the square, taking their prisoner with them. But a mob had been formed during this struggle, and when it invaded the square the foreigners had to fall back before a volley of stones and brickbats to the comparative security of their factories. What might then have happened if the Canton authorities had not intervened is a matter of conjecture. Feeling was running high on both sides. Fortunately, word of the riot had been carried to Houqua, and at his instigation a detachment of Chinese troops was sent to the rescue of the beleaguered foreigners. The rioters, whose numbers had by then swelled to some eight or ten thousand, were driven from the square with whips.

It had been an exciting day. Consul Peter W. Snow later reported to his Government that the mob was raised by 'the imprudence and folly of a small number of English and American young men,' and this interpretation of the incident is backed up by Hunter's lament that the Chinese had been driven off. The ground in front of the factories, he wrote, was strewn with broken bottles, and the English and Americans were waiting with keen anticipation the effect of this precaution upon the bare feet of their assailants. Others among the foreigners took the affair more seriously and judged the attempted execution as a wanton interference with their right to consider the foreign settlement private property. We find, for instance, that Charles W. King, of Olyphant and Company, took part in the attack upon the executioners despite his firm's strong opposition to the opium traffic.

To the protests which were filed by the foreigners with the Canton officials, the Viceroy replied bitterly, 'What have you, Foreigners, to do with this question, whether convicted persons shall be executed there or not?' Apparently as far as he was concerned it was a purely rhetorical question. For a few months later another Chinese opium trader was successfully strangled on the very spot where the riot had started. The foreigners' answer this time was simply to strike their national flags, a gesture which it may be doubted was of serious concern to the Canton authorities.

These were but rumblings of the storm which was to break when in March, 1839, the famous Lin Tsê-hsü, specially named by the Emperor as High Commissioner for the suppression of the opium trade, reached Canton. He came armed with full powers and determined to enforce the laws, not only against the Chinese dealers, but against the foreigners. Less than a week after his arrival, he issued a fair, logical, and vigorous edict demanding the immediate surrender of all opium in the possession of the foreign traders and the signature within three days of a bond guaranteeing that there would be no further importation of the forbidden drug.

The opium trade had grown to such an extent, Lin declared, that the foreigners were 'steeped to the lips in gain,' while in his celestial retreat at Peking the Emperor 'actually quivers with indignation.' The significance of the execution of the Chinese dealers was carefully pointed out, 'not bearing to slay you without previous instructive warning,' but it was impressed upon the foreigners that violation of the required bond 'never to all eternity to dare to bring any opium,' would be punished by confiscation of the offending vessel and the death of its crew. If his orders were met, all would be forgiven; otherwise the trade would be cut off altogether and the foreigners driven away.

This was a different type of proclamation from those which the foreigners had been in the custom of disregarding so carelessly. Lin meant business. And this the residents at Canton were soon to discover when, making common cause, although the issue was one which almost wholly concerned the British, they refused to comply with the Commissioner's demands.

At once trade was stopped, the Chinese servants were withdrawn from the factories, troops concentrated in the suburbs, and warships drawn up along the water-front. The foreign settlement was in a virtual state of siege with guards with drawn swords posted at every entrance. Lin loaded the hong merchants with chains and threatened to execute them if they did not persuade the barbarian traders to surrender.

As for the foreigners, they seem to have accepted their dangerous situation with considerable equanimity. They had become so convinced of the security accorded them by the Chinese Government that even Lin's display of force could not persuade them that any violent measures would be taken against them.

There was never a merrier community than that at Canton during the period of imprisonment, wrote R. B. Forbes. Apparently the Americans thoroughly enjoyed working out the domestic problem presented by the sudden disappearance of all their servants, and since the hong merchants surreptitiously sent them in supplies, despite Lin's strict orders, they did not want for plenty to eat. The chief trouble at their hong seems to have been the problem of finding some one skilled enough to act as cook. Forbes himself started out in this capacity, but sadly writes that he was soon deposed. The other jobs in Chinese house-keeping were successfully filled, with certain of the dignified China merchants ably acting as dishwashers, bedmakers, or house-cleaners, while the members of their staffs, as Hunter wrote, 'from a feeling of modesty or a feeling of sheer incapacity, did no more than was absolutely necessary.'

This state of affairs lasted for about a week, with Lin still holding the whole community in close confinement and the foreigners cut off from all communications with the outside world, when the British Superintendent of Trade, Captain Charles Elliot, who had vainly attempted to secure his countrymen's liberty, found himself forced to take action. The great bulk of the opium which the Chinese demanded was British property, and he did not feel himself justified on its account in jeopardizing not only the foreign trade but the lives and property of all foreigners in Canton. Therefore he surrendered. He agreed to hand over to the Chinese authorities 20,280 chests of opium, of which 1540 were held, but on account of the English, by Americans.

When this opium was delivered and taken in charge by the Chinese, the siege of the foreign settlement was raised, but only one of Lin's demands had been met. The Chinese Commissioner had won a dramatic victory by forcing the surrender of the opium; he intended to insist just as strenuously on the signature of the bond against any further importation.

On this point the English attitude was just as determined as his own. Captain Elliot had given up the opium only as a matter of expediency because he felt foreign lives were endangered, but as an official representative of Great Britain, he had no intention of admitting that the Chinese were right in principle in this confiscation of personal property, or that they could in such summary fashion enforce their laws upon British subjects. He ordered all the English merchants to withdraw from Canton and give up their trade, while he reserved the right for his Government to demand an indemnity for the surrendered opium.

With the Americans the situation was quite different. They had not been forced to give up any opium of their own — Hunter declares that they had only fifty chests which the Chinese might have demanded — and they were not vitally interested in the opium trade. In fact, its abolition would have been greatly to their advantage, for it would have increased the market at Canton for other goods and aided their trade at the expense of that of the British. They had no reason to make an issue of the present controversy, and, as in every previous crisis with the Chinese authorities, all that they sought was the restoration of peaceful relations and the opportunity to continue their normal and lawful commerce.

The bond which Commissioner Lin presented to the American Consul for signature in behalf of his nationals did, however, present difficulties. It stipulated that should any opium at all be found upon an American vessel, the ship would be liable to confiscation and its entire crew liable to death. The Consul, moreover, was to be held responsible for his countrymen's behavior.

Consul Peter W. Snow was ready to promise that there would be no more American imports of opium, but the penalties of this bond were too severe. He refused to have anything to do with it, and instead urged the Americans to withdraw from Canton as had the English. At the same time he suggested, in his report to Washington on the events of the past six weeks, that the time now seemed opportune to attempt to negotiate a commercial treaty with China, and that it might be well to afford the trade some measure of naval protection.

He had, however, no authority over the American merchants, and they had no intention of injuring their position in Canton by further association with the English in a cause which was no concern of theirs. They did not sign Lin's original bond, but were easily induced to sign a second in modified form, by which they solemnly bound themselves to have nothing further to do with the opium traffic. This satisfied the Chinese Commissioner, and despite the urging of the British and of their own Consul, the American merchants were soon carrying on their interrupted trade as if nothing had happened.

As Forbes pointed out, his countrymen were 'under no control, subject to no law, except that of self-interest.' And even more succinct is his statement of their position as made to Captain Elliot when the latter asked Russell and Company to withdraw from Canton in support of the British traders. He had not come to China for health or pleasure, Forbes told the English official, and he intended to remain at his post as long as he could 'sell a yard of goods or buy a pound of tea.'

At first the British traders, having retired to their merchant fleet, which was anchored idle and disconsolate off the island of Hongkong, greatly resented this attitude upon the part of the Americans. They saw their trade snatched out of their hands, their rivals on more than ever friendly terms with the Chinese, while they had broken off all relations. But soon they realized that the American commerce might also be to their advantage. The authority of their Superintendent of Trade might prevent them from returning to Canton, but it could not keep them from using the Americans as middlemen to save as much of their trade as they could. They hired American ships to freight their goods back and forth between Hongkong and Canton, even selling some of their own that they might operate under the American flag, and coöperated as much as possible to get out the season's tea crop before the possible outbreak of open hostilities between England and China.

The activity of the American vessels during this period of neither peace nor war between China and England was tremendous. They were towed up and down the river with cotton or tea piled eight and ten feet high on the decks. Even the spars were taken down to lessen the vessels' weight. If the Chinese objected to their carrying British goods, though in time they came to realize that the freighting done by the Americans was as much to their advantage as to that of the English, short trips would be made to Manila or Batavia to keep up the fiction that it was *bona fide* American trade.

In this way the entire commerce of Canton was carried on for the rest of the season, with the Americans reaping a rich harvest in freight' rates, which were higher for the ninety-mile run between Whampoa and Hongkong than they ordinarily were from China to the United States. The Americans took full advantage of the position in which they found themselves, but the English also profited by this freighting trade. Elliot himself came in time to recognize this, and finally told Forbes that 'the Queen owes you many thanks for not taking my advice as to leaving Canton.'

# CHAPTER XI

## ANGLO–CHINESE HOSTILITIES

THE situation in Canton toward the close of 1839 could not have been more confused. The English were still holding out resolutely against the signature of any bond imposing those extreme penalties for the further importation of opium which had been proposed by Commissioner Lin, but at the same time they were trading actively with the Chinese merchants through the medium of American ships. The Chinese still refused to withdraw from the position they had assumed and the members of the co-hong were forbidden to trade with the English, but they also were glad to take advantage of the facilities for trade offered by the Americans. In both cases principle was warring against commercial interests. Victory might have gone to the latter had it not been that behind the immediate cause of the Anglo-Chinese controversy lurked the one important question which could not be settled by compromise: that is, international equality.

But if that principle lay at the bottom of the quarrel between the English and the Chinese, it was nevertheless a series of minor incidents which brought matters to a head and resulted in actual war. For one thing, the trade in opium started up again. Before the Chinese had destroyed the surrendered chests, it was renewed by the British dealers, and Captain Elliot, who had done what he could to keep the opium ships from Lintin, reported to his Government that 'a most vigorous trade is carried on at places about two hundred miles to the eastward of Canton.' A few months later, a similar statement was made in the 'Chinese

Repository.' The opium traffic, it declared, 'seems to be as vigorously prosecuted as ever, and with as much safety and profit.'[1]

This open disregard of the reform which the Chinese were honestly trying to enforce naturally served to increase their resentment against the British, while at the same time two further complications occurred which stiffened their attitude and shut the door to possible compromise. The first of these was the death of a Chinese, one Lin Wei-hi, in a drunken affray between some Chinese villagers and English sailors on the island of Kowloon; the second was the action of the British ship *Thomas Coutts*, which calmly disregarded Captain Elliot's order for an embargo on all trade and proceeded to sign the bond required by Commissioner Lin. If the one incident brought up the old controversial question of Chinese jurisdiction over the foreigners, the other convinced the authorities at Canton that if they held out long enough the self-interest of the English traders would induce them to follow the example of the captain of the *Thomas Coutts* and compel Captain Elliot to surrender.

The British official had no such idea. He was more than ever persuaded of the necessity of forcing things to an issue. Hostilities, in fact, were not far distant. In November, a force of twenty-nine war junks swept down upon the English merchant fleet anchored off Hongkong to demand the surrender of Lin Wei-hi's murderer. Captain Elliot did not know the murderer, and in any event had no intention of handing any English sailor over to Chinese justice. This he told the admiral in command of the junks, and when the latter continued to advance upon the English fleet, he took decisive action. The British ships opened fire,

---

[1] Consul Snow reported, on September 23, 1839, that at that time there were no Americans in the opium trade, despite British activity.

and after blowing up four of the junks, they forced the rest to retire. It was war.

None of these events had any effect upon the Americans. They continued to trade as best they could throughout 1839 and even in the succeeding years of actual war. They were constantly protesting against any British attempt to blockade Canton. For the handful of traders who remained in the Chinese city, the slogan which they preached, and on which they invariably acted, was 'Business as usual.'

Before hostilities had broken out, eight of these American merchants had sent a memorial to Washington suggesting that the time had come for united action on the part of England, France, Holland, and the United States to induce the Chinese to increase foreign trading privileges, but they did not really expect their Government to intervene.[1] They do not seem to have been vitally interested in the matter themselves, and certainly not to the extent of wishing to run the risk of inviting Chinese hostility. Some of them had little confidence in such British aims as the opening of new ports to foreign trade. They were, by and large, content with conditions as they had been before Commissioner Lin and Captain Elliot had brought affairs to a crisis.

The scene now shifts to London, where the imminence of war resulted in the inevitable parliamentary debates. The policy of the Government in allowing Chinese relations to drift into such a serious *impasse* was vigorously attacked, but events had gone so far that the necessity of using force

---

[1] Some comfort had been afforded the Americans by the opportune arrival, in the very midst of the excitement of their imprisonment at Canton, of two American ships of war, the frigate *Columbia* and the sloop *John Adams*, under the command of Commodore Read. But the naval officer had agreed with the Consul that the bond required by the Chinese should not be signed. When trade had been resumed, the squadron thereupon left Canton, in the face of frantic protests from the mercantile community.

to uphold British prestige was generally accepted. No one advocated war because of the seizure of the opium, but the trade in the contraband drug was condoned and Palmerston maintained that the Chinese were not sincere in their efforts to suppress it. The Opposition might express grave doubts as to whether the case of the Chinese was not actually stronger than that of the British, but a division along purely party lines upheld the Government and Lord John Russell, Secretary of State for the Colonies, declared that war had been 'set afoot to obtain reparation for insults and injuries offered Her Majesty's superintendent and subjects; to obtain indemnification for the losses the merchants had sustained under threat of violence; and, lastly, to get security that persons and property trading with China should in future be protected from insult and injury, and trade maintained upon a proper footing.'

No official declaration of war was ever made by either Great Britain or China. Commissioner Lin had sent a characteristically bombastic declaration to Queen Victoria. 'You savages of the further seas,' he pompously wrote, 'have waxed so bold, it seems, as to defy and insult our mighty Empire. Of a truth it is high time for you to "flay the face and cleanse the heart," and to amend your ways. If you submit humbly to the Celestial dynasty and tender your allegiance, it may give you a chance to purge yourself of your past sins. But if you continue and persist in your path of obstinate delusion, your three islands will be laid waste and your people pounded into mincemeat, so soon as the armies of his Divine Majesty set foot upon your shores.'

Great Britain's answer was also characteristic. An Order in Council was adopted to obtain 'satisfaction and reparation for the late injurious proceedings,' and sixteen ships of war carrying five hundred and forty guns, four steamers, one troopship, twenty-seven transports, and four thousand land forces were immediately dispatched to Chinese waters.

Official operations against the Chinese were initiated with a blockade of the river and port of Canton on June 28, 1840, but the orders brought out from England by Admiral George Elliot, who had been appointed British Commissioner jointly with his cousin Captain Elliot, were to carry the war to the north and open negotiations directly with Peking for settlement of Great Britain's grievances. Consequently, Tinghai, capital of the island of Chusan off the coast of Chekiang, was occupied, and, after blockading Ningpo and the mouth of the Yangtze, the British fleet took up its position at the Peiho River near Tientsin.

The Chinese had been powerless before this display of force and had no means of resisting the advance of the British war vessels. They were ready to sue for peace. Negotiations were entered into by Captain Elliot and Viceroy Kishen of the Province of the Chihli, which resulted in a convention whereby the Chinese agreed to surrender Hongkong to the British, pay an indemnity of six million dollars, open trade at Canton, and permit direct official intercourse between England and China on terms of absolute equality.

This settlement satisfied no one. The war party at Peking, merely slow at getting into action, was still far from convinced of Britain's obvious superiority in war, and the Emperor was besieged with memorials urging him to renew hostilities and drive the impudent foreign devils into the sea. The vainglorious mandarins of the capital, whose pride was equaled only by their ignorance, were convinced that the Emperor had but to show the real strength of his ever-victorious armies for the barbarians to flee. They were far from ready to submit to the humiliation of the peace which the British would have forced upon them.

Nor were the English content with the convention signed by Captain Elliot. Having once started upon war, the Government was determined to carry it through to the point where full satisfaction was secured. If from the Chinese point of view the convention granted far too much, from that of the British it granted far too little.

Captain Elliot had ended the occupation of Chusan, which had taken a heavy toll in English lives through sickness, and was prepared to open the trade at Canton, but the war party at Peking soon forced his hand. The Emperor ordered a concentration of troops at Tinghai and at Canton to 'destroy and wipe clean away, to exterminate and root out the rebellious barbarians... beings that the overshadowing vault and all-containing earth can hardly suffer to live.' A 'majesty-bearing generalissimo' supported by 'rebel-quelling generals' took the field, and high rewards were offered for the capture of British ships and of Englishmen, dead or alive.

Commodore Sir Gordon Bremer, who had now succeeded Admiral Elliot in charge of the fleet, thereupon moved up the Pearl River. The Bogue forts were captured and seventy-one war junks and shore batteries mounting over sixty guns were destroyed in a general engagement off the foreign factories. Preparations were then made for an assault upon Canton itself with artillery and infantry, when at the last moment the Chinese merchants of the city offered to pay a ransom of six million dollars to save it from attack. Captain Elliot, still anxious for peace and zealous in the interests of the tea trade, accepted this offer.

This was in May, 1841. Within a few weeks Colonel Sir Henry Pottinger and Rear-Admiral Sir William Parker reached China with commissions to supersede those of both Captain Elliot and Commodore Bremer. Palmerston was discontented with the somewhat dilatory tactics of Captain Elliot and determined to push things through. His instructions to Sir Henry Pottinger were to reoccupy Chusan, force new negotiations at the mouth of the Peiho, and secure in full Great Britain's aims. National interests were no longer to be subordinated to those of commerce.

The war then entered a second and far more vigorous phase. Again the British fleet started north with 2519 troops. Amoy, Tinghai, Chinhai, and Ningpo were captured in rapid succession. The Chinese were at the mercy of the invaders. They could do nothing. At times they put up a brave resistance and fought valiantly, but their lack of discipline, their unfamiliarity with the tactics of modern warfare, and their want of weapons left them helpless before the onslaughts of the trained and well-equipped British forces.

The courage and desperation of the Manchu garrisons, whose scorn and hatred of the foreign barbarian made any fate more desirable than that of falling alive into his hands, often resulted in scenes of tragic heroism such as the English soldiers had never witnessed or imagined. At Chapu the garrison stood to its post until not only were the troops decimated, but the women and children had been offered to the sword in order to prevent their falling into the enemies' hands. More than twelve thousand persons perished, either in the attack of the English or by their own swords, in an action in which the invaders lost but nine.

At Chinkiang, where the steady advance of the British next carried the war, even more desperate scenes were enacted. 'Such was their terror and hatred of the invaders,' writes S. Wells Williams in 'The Middle Kingdom,' 'that

THE CAPTURE OF TING-HAI, CHUSAN

every Manchu preferred resistance, death, suicide, or flight
to surrender. Out of a Manchu population of four thousand,
it was estimated that not more than five hundred survived,
the greater part having perished by their own hands.' The
throats of the women were cut and babies thrown into wells
to save them from what the Manchus regarded as the far
worse fate of capture.

It was only after Shanghai had fallen and an assault had
been ordered against Nanking that the imperial court
recognized the inevitable and accepted the British terms.
The Chinese had at last been forced to recognize that their
country's claims to world superiority could not be supported and that the Son of Heaven no longer could exact
tribute from the Western Ocean nations. The haughty and
insolent self-esteem of the Manchus had been ruthlessly
punctured by British bayonets. War had succeeded where
diplomacy had failed. When China sued for peace, the day
when the foreign devils could be treated with impudent
scorn had come to a disastrous end.

Neither Commissioner Lin, who had brought this war
upon China, nor Commissioner Kishen, who had signed the
first articles of peace, were empowered to treat with the
English. They had paid the price the Son of Heaven always exacted for failure. The latter had been degraded and
exiled; the former left Canton in chains and was transported
to the Amur. 'You have not only proved yourself unable to
cut off their trade,' read the imperial edict, 'but you have
proved yourself unable to seize perverse natives. You have
but dissembled with empty words, and so far from having
been any help in the affair, you have caused the waves of
confusion to arise, and a thousand interminable disorders are
sprouting; in fact you have been as if your arms were tied,
without knowing what to do: it appears, then, you are no

better than a wooden image. When I meditate on all these things, I am filled with anger and melancholy.' True it was Lin had sown the tempest and reaped the whirlwind, but he had only followed his orders.

The terms of the British-imposed peace were signed at Nanking aboard H.M.S. *Cornwallis* by Sir Henry Pottinger and three Chinese envoys, Commissioners Kiying and Ilipu and the Nanking Viceroy, Niu Kien, on August 29, 1842. The treaty provided for the cession of Hongkong, the opening of trade at the four additional ports of Shanghai, Amoy, Ningpo, and Foochow, the establishment of British consuls, an indemnity of twenty-one million dollars, of which six million dollars was for the destroyed opium, the abolition of the monopoly of the co-hong as a system of trading, the establishment of a uniform and moderate tariff, and the recognition of absolute equality between China and Great Britain. Nothing was said about the trade in opium.

This was the first Anglo-Chinese war, which has gone down in history as the 'Opium War.' It has been vilified as strongly by British historians as by those of other nationality.[1] Its immediate origin and the circumstances under which it began cannot be very well defended. Yet at the same time it must be admitted that Great Britain had submitted to much provocation in the insolent manner in which China had met all its previous attempts to establish friendly relations, and in so far as it fought to maintain the equality of nations, it was fighting the battle of the Western world. Its great and indefensible mistake was in allowing

---

[1] In his *A History of Our Own Times*, for example, Justin M'Carthy says: '... in the beginning and the very origin of the quarrel we were distinctly in the wrong. We asserted, or at least acted upon the assertion of, a claim so unreasonable and even monstrous that it never could have been made upon any nation strong enough to render its assertion a matter of serious responsibility.'

a crisis to arise over opium, in which the Chinese were clearly and unmistakably in the right. That blot upon the relations between China and the West can never be removed.

In the next chapter contemporary American opinion upon the war will be fully discussed. As for the Americans at Canton, they had been able to hold aloof from the war, maintain their cordial relations with the Chinese, and with some interruptions continue their trade. It was peace which brought new problems. The opportune arrival in Canton of Commodore Lawrence Kearny, of the U.S. Frigate *Constellation*, fortunately gave them an official representative to take up with the Chinese authorities the changed conditions of trade as effected by the Treaty of Nanking.

Commodore Kearny had arrived in Chinese waters some few months before the end of the war and proceeding up the Pearl River, the first American warship to pass the Bogue, he found a situation quite different from that which any former American naval officer had ever experienced. Thanks to the salutary lesson which the Chinese had learned from their struggle with the British, foreigners were now treated with something akin to respect. Relations between Commodore Kearny and the Canton officials were established automatically and an entirely amicable correspondence was carried on without reference to the hong merchants. A Chinese admiral even paid a formal visit to the *Constellation* and was greeted by an official salute and the manning of the yards. The day of frantic proclamations forbidding foreign war vessels to 'loiter about' had passed.

Almost the first thing done by Commodore Kearny upon his arrival was to issue through the United States Consul an announcement that his Government would not sanction any opium smuggling under the American flag. What is more, he meant it. The American merchants were warned against the risks such a course would entail, and before he left the China coast the Commodore gave even greater point to his declaration of policy by forcing the schooner *Ariel* to dispose of an illegal cargo and depriving her of her American papers. In view of the somewhat equivocal attitude of the British, it is no wonder that the Canton Viceroy hailed this friendly act and even went so far as to declare — with evident exaggeration — that the American ships had always obeyed the law.

Commodore Kearny next entered a protest against an incident of the previous year which had resulted in the death of one American and the injury of several others when the Chinese had fired upon a boat of the ship *Morrison*. The reply was most conciliatory. The Chinese official explained that the Americans had been mistaken for English, and as soon as their identity had become known, every attempt had been made to make restitution for the unwarranted attack. Commodore Kearny was requested to fix an indemnity for the outrage in conference with the hong merchants and eventually the American claims were fully met by a payment of seventy-eight hundred dollars.

The points at issue between the Americans and Chinese were thus satisfactorily settled. Direct communications with the Viceroy were allowed, commercial relations were on a most favorable footing, and the American flag was respected. Still Commodore Kearny was not satisfied. Peace having been agreed upon by China and Great Britain, he was anxiously concerned to know if the new privileges granted to the English would also be extended to the Americans. Consequently, on October 8, 1842, he wrote to Commissioner Kiying, who was also Governor of Canton, expressing the hope that American interests would not be overlooked in the new arrangements for foreign commerce and that the trade and citizens of the United States would be 'placed upon the same footing as the merchants of the nation most favored.'

The prompt reply to this communication was all that the American envoy could have expected. Kiying promised that the matter would be taken up at once. 'Decidedly it shall not be permitted,' he wrote, 'that the American merchants shall come to have merely a dry stick.'

In this somewhat cryptic statement may be found the genesis of the most-favored-nation doctrine as applied to China's foreign relations, which in turn was to form the foundation of the open-door policy. The line of development from this exchange of letters between Commodore Kearny and Commissioner Kiying to the reassertion of the open door by Secretary Hay some fifty-seven years later is clear and direct.

It is true that a year earlier Captain Elliot had announced that the British sought no special individual privileges in their attack upon China, but nevertheless there was nothing in the treaty which they eventually signed to indicate that they expected the Americans to share in all the rights secured to them by war. It was action by the Chinese themselves, as foreshadowed in this statement by Kiying, which assured for the Americans their equal rights in the new China trade. Naturally it was a question in which the merchants of the United States were vitally concerned, for no matter what their feelings might be in regard to the Anglo-Chinese War, they could not stand by and see their position in China completely undermined. They had not fought for the opening of the new treaty ports and the granting of new privileges, but if they were to be secured by the British it was essential that they be enjoyed by the United States.

That the Chinese were prepared to admit these claims is a tribute to their political sagacity, and it subsequently developed that they had officially provided for such action even earlier than was at first realized. In a treaty with England supplementary to the Treaty of Nanking, signed at the Bogue on October 8, 1843, the Chinese text differed somewhat from the English in stating that 'the merchants of the various nations of Europe should be allowed to proceed to the four ports of Foochow, Ningpo, Amoy, and Shanghai for the purposes of trade, to which the English were not to make any objections....'

In all events, Commodore Kearny now felt that American rights were fully protected, and he would have left Canton had not the American Consul and American merchants prevailed upon him to remain until conditions became somewhat more settled. His presence was effective in securing indemnification of $253,430 for American property destroyed in the riots which broke out in Canton toward the close of 1842. Then before he left the China coast he again took up the question of American trading privileges, as at that time it still seemed uncertain whether the new ports were really going to be open to all foreigners.

On this occasion the Chinese officials referred to his communication as a request 'to solicit the favor of the Emperor,' and suggested that if the Imperial Commissioner and the Commodore could meet 'face to face, the relations between the two countries may be arranged.' Commodore Kearny detected in this reply a recrudescence of Chinese superiority. His answer was that the United States was seeking equal treatment, not as a favor, but as a right, and that the Emperor should appoint high commissioners to negotiate a special treaty with similar officials of the United States.

This was not exactly the Chinese idea. Further treaties with the foreigners were not altogether to their liking, and the answer given to Commodore Kearny was that the accord he proposed 'would be an unnecessary and circuitous act.' Nevertheless, it was again emphasized that the Americans would not be shut off from the privileges granted to the English, and it was definitely stated that 'the various particulars relating to the commercial duties to be paid by each country are all to be regulated uniformly by one rule, without the least partiality to be manifested towards any one.'

Here was a written promise supplementing Kiying's first acknowledgment of American rights and pointing the way to the subsequent treaty which the United States was to negotiate to counterbalance the treaties signed by Great Britain. Commodore Kearny could leave Canton content. By bringing up the question at the opportune moment, he had assured for the United States, without a single hostile act, those same privileges which the English had won after hostilities extending over almost three years. What is more, the traditional friendship of the Americans and the Chinese had not been sacrificed one iota.

The first accounts of the early relations between the United States and China painted a satisfying picture of American kindness and forbearance toward the Chinese as contrasted with the aggressive and warlike attitude of the British. More lately the pendulum has swung the other way. We have a picture of the United States selfishly holding aloof while the British fought its battles, and then rushing in to demand for itself the privileges which the British had won through so many sacrifices in the common cause.

Neither picture would seem to be entirely true. The United States did not concern itself with the first Anglo-Chinese war because its interests were not vitally affected. The Americans at Canton were the only ones concerned and they were on the whole satisfied with the conditions under which they were allowed to trade, and opposed to the traffic in opium. For entirely selfish reasons — the continuance of their trade — they were consequently more friendly than the British toward the Chinese and more willing to submit to the petty annoyances and vexations to which the merchants of both nations were subjected by the haughty mandarins of Canton. They might have favored a joint exhibition of force to convince the Chinese of the respect due to foreigners, but they opposed war.

Nevertheless, once the war had been fought and the British had secured new trading privileges, the United States could not stand by and see its trade still confined to the old channels. That would have been practically impossible. It would have caused the withdrawal of the Americans from China altogether, because they could not possibly have competed with their privileged rivals. It is easy to see — as the Chinese quickly recognized — that it was as much to the interest of China as to that of the United States that the position of England should not be favored above that of other Western nations.

Self-interest was entirely responsible for the first flowering of the open-door policy in China. But there is no reason why this should discredit a development which first cast America in the rôle of friend to China, and subsequently was to check her division into separate spheres of foreign influence.

# CHAPTER XII

## THE CUSHING COMMISSION

ALTHOUGH an ocean and a continent separated the Canton outpost of American trade from the United States Government, the reverberations of the Anglo-Chinese War soon reached Washington. None of the other vicissitudes through which the merchants had passed in far-off China had made any impression upon the official American consciousness, but once dispatches reached home that England was fighting a war and winning new commercial privileges, Congress demanded that the Government investigate the conditions under which the American traders were operating.

It was not that the China trade had been ignored at home. Ever since the voyage of the *Empress of China* had first opened up the route to the Far East, the traffic in silks and tea had kept its romantic appeal for all those interested in foreign commerce. New York, Philadelphia, Boston, and Salem had been too intimately bound up with the trade's development not to feel a certain kinship with Canton. Many of the mercantile fortunes of these cities were founded upon tea, and Massachusetts had owed its economic revival after the Revolution in a large measure to commerce beyond the Cape of Good Hope. For decades the long, hazardous voyages to the Pacific had constituted the training school for our merchant marine and attracted the most far-sighted merchants, the finest ships, and the most able seamen in the country's growing commerce.

The trade with the Northwest Coast, moreover, had led to the discovery of the Columbia River and the first settlements in Oregon. On these events were based America's claim to the Northwest territory, and it was because of the potentialities of the China trade that we refused to abandon our rights to a part of the continent which was at first desired simply as a base for commercial activities in the Pacific. When the Oregon question was debated in Congress in 1822, the Northwest Coast was not thought of as a vast territory to be opened up for settlement by American frontiersmen. It was discussed as the great *entrepôt* for commerce with China, and it was even suggested that it should be populated with Chinese who might produce goods for the Canton market. A water route across the continent to the Columbia River, with New York, Albany, and Sandusky its post-towns, was the bright prospect held out, not only for American trade with China, but for British trade with India.

Even as late as 1844 these ideas were advanced as the compelling reason for standing by our guns in the long controversy with England, which was finally settled two years later with the acceptance of the forty-ninth parallel as the Northwest boundary. Addressing the Senate, Senator Breese urged support for our claims to the Northwest because developments in China were opening up a rich market for cotton and tobacco which might be shipped to the Far East by the Missouri and Columbia Rivers.

So, too, had interest in China been awakened by other branches of the commerce. The startling tales of seamen who had fought off treacherous Indian tribes in Nootka Sound were matched by the stories of hardship and danger among the Seal Islands and even more glamorous accounts of adventures in the South Seas. From Canton itself merchants and sea captains brought home unfamiliar tales of a land strange and mysterious. The foreign factories squatting on the river-bank beside the walls of a city which no foreigner

was allowed to enter, the haughty mandarins overwhelming
the outside barbarians with their celestial scorn, the dignified and open-handed merchants of the co-hong, whose word
was their bond and whose honesty was above reproach,
made up a picture of China which had been deeply impressed upon the mind of America.

Tea was a part of every American's daily life and it came
from nowhere but China. Nankeens may have been forgotten with New England's growing manufacture of cotton
goods; silks and Canton crapes may have somewhat waned
in popularity with changing fashions, but they had made
Chinese goods familiar throughout the country. The table-
ware which had replaced the pewter dishes of the colonists
actually bore the name of this far-off country.

Such evidences of American interest in China might be
multiplied almost indefinitely. There was the prompt publication in the United States of the journals of Lord Macartney's embassy to the Son of Heaven, the popularity of
the accounts of voyages to China published by American
travelers, the vogue for curios brought home from Canton,
and the exhibition in a New York theater of a Chinese girl
whose tightly bound feet created a nine-day sensation.
Then, in 1839, the Chinese Museum of Nathan Dunn was
established in Philadelphia. It was a collection of curiosities portraying every phase of life in Canton. Life-size
figures in Chinese costumes, models of streets and houses,
scenes of manufacturing and farming, examples of handiwork of Chinese artisans, made the thousands of visitors
who passed through the Museum more familiar with China
than are many Americans to-day.

Missionary enterprise in the Far East was inaugurated
when the Reverend David Abeel and the Reverend Elijah
C. Bridgman were sent to Canton in 1829, to be shortly

followed by such well-known figures as S. Wells Williams and Dr. Peter Parker. From then on church circles became as interested in China as were commercial circles. The opium smuggling excited tremendous concern for the welfare of the benighted heathen of far Cathay, and throughout the country the discussion raged as to what should be done to bring the Chinese within the fold of Western civilization.

If, despite all this popular interest in things Chinese, no Government action other than the casual appointment of consuls was taken to promote the trade at Canton or to establish more direct relations between China and the United States, the reason is not far to seek. Young America had too many other problems to concern itself officially with anything so far off. The period of the old China trade was primarily a period of national expansion. War and continued quarrels with Great Britain, long-drawn-out negotiations with France for settlement of American claims against French privateers, the purchase of Louisiana and the acquisition of Florida, endless fighting with the Indians as the frontiersmen pushed steadily westward across the continent, may well have absorbed the interests of those charged with the conduct of foreign policy to the exclusion of anything so remote as our relations with an empire on the other side of the world.

About 1840, there were even more reasons why America should not become greatly excited over problems in the Far East. Controversy with Great Britain over boundaries both in the Northeast and the Northwest had led to a dangerous state of friction between the two countries. But the most pressing question before the United States was its attitude toward Texas, which had broken away from Mexico to become an independent state.[1] The annexation

---

The British representative in Texas in 1842 was none other than Captain Charles Elliot, fresh from his troubled experiences in Canton.

issue was becoming all-important at Washington. The way was being prepared for the Mexican War, and the wonder is that under these conditions even hostilities in China could spur Congress to look so far afield.

Its first intimation of the direction events were taking in China had been the memorial of the eight American merchants resident in Canton, who, in 1839, urged that the United States take common action with Great Britain, France, and Holland to establish a new basis for commercial intercourse. Their idea was to make a direct appeal to Peking for permanent residence of foreign envoys at the imperial court, for a fixed tariff, bonded warehouses, the opening of new ports to trade, compensation for the stoppage of legal trade, and for an agreement that the Chinese should mete out no punishment for the crimes of foreigners more severe than similar offenses would entail under British or American law. Should the Government not favor such a programme, the merchants asked that an American commissioner be sent to China and naval protection accorded their trade.

A few months later, Thomas H. Perkins and a group of Massachusetts merchants in the China trade submitted a somewhat similar memorial, except that the idea of co-operation with the British had been abandoned and a more cautious tone adopted. They, too, urged that a naval force be sent to the Far East, but warned against any action which might lead the Chinese to associate Americans with the British in the impending war. The Government was advised to move slowly in any attempt to negotiate with China, and the idea of sending an envoy to Peking was opposed on the ground that Great Britain had never found such procedure very satisfactory.

These memorials may have been responsible for the dispatch of Commodore Kearny to Canton, but otherwise they had no immediate results. It was obvious that the state of American relations with Great Britain made any form of coöperation between the two countries impossible, even if it had been otherwise desirable. All that Congress felt itself obligated to do in 1840 was to pass two resolutions for inquiries into the Chinese situation, one asking the President to render a full report on American commerce at Canton, and the other requesting a résumé of all relations between China and the United States since the opening of the trade.

In the mean time war had commenced in China, and American opinion soon showed itself bitterly opposed to British policy. Some idea of this may be gained from articles in 'Niles' Register,' which had for many years shown a special interest in Chinese affairs, colored by a bitter anti-British policy. As early as 1822, during one of the periodic quarrels between the English and Chinese, it assailed England's refusal to abide by Chinese law and pointed out that Great Britain had little right to complain of Chinese severity when its own laws provided hanging for a person convicted of snaring a rabbit. Answering a British suggestion that Canton should be captured to forward the 'acquisition of a barbarous wilderness into the pale of civilization,' it had savagely attacked the idea as a 'tissue of rapine, robbery, religious cant, and hypocrisy.' The theory of forcing trade on China, this article declared, might just as well be applied by the United States to the West Indies, where its interests had clashed with those of Great Britain.

The events of 1840, of course, added even more fuel to this fire, and England's alleged greed for power and cupidity for trade called forth the most bitter comment. China did not commend itself to the editors of 'Niles' Register' by allowing itself to become the quiet victim of Great Britain's attack, but Europe was assailed for standing by with folded arms and 'not even breathing the cheap objection of a manifesto against this new evidence of rapacity.'

This widespread feeling was reflected by Caleb Cushing, who had introduced the first resolution into Congress for an inquiry into the China trade, in a speech he felt called upon to make in explanation of his motives. There was no idea in his proposal, he told Congress, of joining England in the war against China. Quite the contrary. It was the Americans almost alone among the foreigners at Canton who had manifested a proper respect for the laws and public rights of the Chinese Empire 'in honorable contrast with the outrageous misconduct of the British there.' He felt that this was a favorable time to attempt to stabilize trade, 'but God forbid that I should entertain the idea of coöperating with the British Government in the purpose, if purpose it has, of upholding the base cupidity and violence and high-handed infraction of all law, human and divine, which have characterized the operations of the British, individually and collectively, in the seas of China.'

Cushing conveniently forgot that American traders had to a certain extent shared in the opium traffic, but for all its violence his speech probably represented public opinion at home on how such trade was regarded. Having received from the chairman of the House Foreign Relations Committee assurances that no form of coöperation with the British was contemplated by the Government, he then declared that England could no longer hope, 'if she chose to persevere in the attempt to coerce the Chinese by force of arms to submit to be poisoned with opium in whole provinces, that she is to receive aid or countenance from the United States in that nefarious enterprise.'

Amid this chorus of disapproval for Great Britain's action, one voice was raised in her support. It was that of John Quincy Adams, who had been Secretary of State at the time of the Terranova case. First in a public address before the Massachusetts Historical Society, which the 'North American Review' refused to print, so high was feeling against Great Britain, and then before Congress, he vigorously advanced the theory that the cause of the war between England and China was not opium, but the latter nation's boasted superiority over every other nation in the world.

Adams pointed out that the fundamental principle of the Chinese Empire was anti-commercial, and that it held itself 'equal to the heavenly host,' while all other nations were considered tributary barbarians which should at all times be 'reverently submissive to the will of its despotic chief.' He refused to accept such a theory, and in thundering terms told his startled audience that 'it is high time that this enormous outrage upon rights of human nature, and upon the first principle of the rights of nations, should cease....'

Declaring that the seizure of the opium was a mere incident in the Anglo-Chinese quarrel and no more the cause of war than the Boston tea party had been the cause of the Revolution, he concluded his address with the emphatic statement that 'the cause of the war is the *kotow!* — the arrogant and insupportable pretensions of China that she will hold commercial intercourse with the rest of mankind, not upon terms of equal reciprocity, but upon the insulting and degrading forms of relation between lord and vassal.'

Adams's views were, of course, far nearer the truth than those of any of his contemporaries. He was better informed on the situation in Canton, and as Secretary of State when Terranova was executed, he must have felt keenly the humiliation which the Americans had undergone at the time of this incident. But in seizing upon the underlying factors which had made the outbreak of hostilities almost inevitable sooner or later, he had chosen to ignore the patent fact that it was the opium seizure which had goaded the British into action. Later he was somewhat to modify his opinion and to speak of the 'questionable morality of the war.' But he continued to maintain, in contrast to those rabid editorial writers who drew a vivid picture of Great Britain forcing opium down the throats of meek and peaceful Chinese at the sword's point, that the struggle was 'in root and substance, for equal rights of independent nations, against the insolent and absurd assumption of despotic supremacy.' [1]

If it had not been for the critical state of Anglo-American relations — in 1841 war seemed imminent — American opinion would undoubtedly have been more influenced by Adams's stand and there would have been more sympathy for British aims. Some hint of this is given in an article in the 'Merchants' Magazine' of March, 1843, which declared that 'however beneficial in its remote consequences the unsealing of the Chinese ports may be, we cannot but regret that it should have been conceived in crime and consummated in violence.'

When peace was concluded between England and China with the signature of the Treaty of Nanking, a more definite proposal than a request for an investigation into conditions

---

[1] Another opponent of the popular view as to the causes of the war was Peter Parker, an American missionary who was later to serve his country in China in various official capacities. He declared that what England sought was simply 'indemnity for the past and security for the future' and that her grounds of dissatisfaction were common to all foreigners in China. A strong advocate of an American mission, his talks in Washington with Adams, Cushing, and Secretary of State Webster undoubtedly influenced the attitude of these men toward the situation which the war had created.

of trade was at length made. Two months after Commodore Kearny had secured in Canton the first promise that American rights would be respected under the new conditions of commerce, Caleb Cushing wrote an interesting letter to President Tyler, which made the specific suggestion that an American mission be sent to China, and showed that Cushing clearly foresaw the advantages to both China and the United States of what was later to become the open-door policy.

He told the President that he had information that the Chinese would be disposed to receive such a mission in a friendly spirit, 'the more so as we only can, by the extent of our commerce, act in counterpoise to that of England, and thus save the Chinese from that which would be extremely inconvenient for them, viz., the condition of being an exclusive monopoly in the hands of England.'

Three days later, on December 30, 1842, President Tyler's message to Congress proposed that a diplomatic agent be accredited to China. He pointed out that with the market for American goods in China having more than doubled within the past ten years, the United States was deeply interested in whether the four additional ports open to British trade would also be open to that of its own ships. Consequently he recommended that an American commissioner should reside in China, watch over all American interests, hold direct intercourse with the Canton officials, and be prepared to address higher functionaries, or the Emperor himself should the occasion arise. This envoy, the President concluded, should be a citizen of weight and intelligence, adequately compensated for his services.

Adams introduced a bill into the House to put this suggestion into effect, which carried an appropriation of forty thousand dollars for the proposed mission. Some objection was raised on the score that the importance of the undertaking did not warrant such a large appropriation, and it was proposed that the status of the commissioner should be simply that of commercial agents in other parts of the world. Fortunately, wiser councils prevailed. It was succinctly pointed out that in the existing state of foreign trade the mission to China was more important than all other similar missions combined, while one Southern Congressman ended his comments on the importance of China as a market for American goods by rhetorically demanding if any one knew 'how much of our tobacco might be there chewed, in place of opium.' The bill then passed by a vote of 96 to 59.

In the Senate the bill ran into politics. President Tyler had incurred the bitter opposition of the Whigs, and his proposal was attacked on purely partisan grounds. Senator Thomas H. Benton argued that the China trade had so far been successful and that there was no need for an expensive mission when relations with the Chinese Government could easily be regularized by instructing a resident merchant to sign a treaty identical with that signed by Great Britain. But his real objection to the China bill was that its appropriation of forty thousand dollars gave the President the power to appoint one of his favorites to a lucrative post without having to submit his name to the Senate. With a sarcastic reference to an American Minister creeping in behind the British Minister to claim the protection of Queen Victoria's petticoats, he declared that the mission had not been created for the country, but for the benefit of one man who was waiting 'to go up and bump his head nineteen times against the ground in order to purchase the privilege of standing up before his Celestial Majesty.'

The mission was authorized at midnight on the last day

of the Senate's session despite these small-minded attacks, and the question then arose as to the appointment of a commissioner. The post was first offered to Edward Everett, American Minister to Great Britain, in supposed pursuit of a scheme hatched by Secretary of State Webster. He was anxious to resign his office, and Everett was to go to China in order to allow him to slip gracefully into the vacated London post. But Everett refused to be forced out of England. President Tyler then turned to Caleb Cushing, who accepted the mission with alacrity.

This appointment, made during the Senatorial recess, more than ever called forth the wrath of the President's enemies. Cushing had deserted the Whigs to become one of Tyler's staunchest supporters and this reward for his treachery to his old party associates excited their bitter resentment. Even Adams referred to Cushing's 'obsequiousness and sacrifice of principle.' There is no question that had the Senate, which had already rejected three times his appointment as Secretary of the Treasury, been in session, he would never have been confirmed as the United States' first Commissioner to China.

For all the political undercurrents in this situation, President Tyler, nevertheless, could not have made a better appointment. Cushing, a shrewd Newburyport, Massachusetts lawyer, was closely identified with the China trade and understood the full significance of the conditions created in Canton by the Anglo-Chinese War. Through his acquaintances among the China merchants and careful study, he was already an expert on Chinese affairs. It was he who had first proposed an inquiry into the trade upon the outbreak of the war and then suggested to President Tyler the establishment of the mission he was destined to head. Moreover, for all his checkered political career, his

shifting allegiances, and his unpopularity, he was a man of
really brilliant talents which showed at their best in the
difficult task he was undertaking. The combination of
firmness and tact which marked his negotiations in China
soon proved that he was an ideal envoy for the inauguration
of our official relations.

Fletcher Webster, son of the Secretary of State, was
appointed secretary to the mission; Dr. Peter Parker and
the Reverend E. C. Bridgman were made its Chinese secretaries; Dr. E. K. Kane was appointed surgeon; and four
young gentlemen were chosen as unpaid attachés, to 'add
dignity and importance to the occasion.'

No presents were to be taken to the Chinese Emperor —
the United States did not wish to be enrolled among the
tribute-bearing nations through a repetition of Lord Macartney's sad experience in 1793 — but a memorandum note in
the archives of the Department of State indicates that the
mission was to be furnished with a comprehensive collection
of scientific objects. They were to include a set of the best
charts, and if possible a globe; a pair of six-shooting pistols,
rifles, etc.; model of war steamer; model of steam excavator;
daguerreotype apparatus ('it can be purchased, perhaps,
in France'); some approved works on fortification, gunnery,
shipbuilding, military and naval strategy, geology, chemis-
try, and the 'Encyclopædia Americana'; a telescope, spy-
glass, barometer, and thermometer; and some useful articles made of India rubber. Against the item 'a model of a
locomotive steam engine, and a plan of railroad,' is the
penciled notation: 'Will require too much time to prepare.
J. T.' [1]

One more impressive touch to the arrangements was the
selection of an official costume for the Commissioner. It

[1] Quoted in Tyler Dennett's *Americans in Eastern Asia.*

was to be the uniform of a major-general: a blue coat with gilt buttons, a white vest, white pantaloons with a gold stripe, and a chapeau with a white plume — the whole with 'some slight additions in the way of embroideries.' This lavishness in costume awoke considerable criticism and caustic reminders of Franklin simplicity. 'Niles' Register' had little confidence in the 'unavailing mummery of courtly style.'

There was little precedent on which the instructions for the mission could be based. The only political relations between the United States and any nations of the East were the treaties with Muscat and Siam which had been negotiated by Edmund Roberts some ten years earlier. They were not very important, had been entered into largely on Roberts's personal initiative rather than because of any demand on the part of American interests, and generally followed the conventional lines of ordinary trade agreements. To cope with the situation in China, the Secretary of State had to strike out along new lines. Consequently he turned for advice to those merchants in the United States who had traded with China.

Their views were summed up in a letter Secretary Webster received from John M. Forbes. It was thought necessary to make some display of force, as the Chinese, Forbes stated, believed that the United States had only two naval vessels. The mission should endeavor to reach the mouth of the Peiho in order to negotiate directly with Peking. The provincial authorities should be warned in advance of the official character of the mission.

On the assumption that the United States was not in any event prepared to force a treaty upon China, the letter ends upon this cautious note: 'If our Envoy does not see his way to *succeed*, let him *do nothing;* let him wait the proper time to act, and if his patience fail, let him be authorized to return home, leaving some member of his mission as *Chargé* to wait an opening.' The American merchants approved the mission, but they did not want it to injure their present position at Canton by any diplomatic conflict with the Chinese Government.

On the basis of such recommendations Secretary Webster drew up the documents which appointed Cushing not only Chinese Commissioner, but Envoy Extraordinary and Minister Plenipotentiary for the negotiation of a treaty which would open to American ships the four ports newly opened to the British. The hope was expressed that the jealousy and repulsive feelings which the Chinese entertained toward foreigners would be removed or at least mitigated by the prudence and address of the Commissioner, and that above all he would be able to convince the Government and people of China of the pacific aims of the United States.

In general terms Cushing was instructed to show respect for the institutions and manners of the Chinese and to demonstrate the intention of the Americans to observe their laws. In specific regard to opium he was to make clear that the United States would not interfere to protect smugglers from the consequences of their own illegal conduct. He had orders to dismiss the American Consul, Paul S. Forbes, if charges that his firm was engaged in the opium traffic should prove to be true.

On the other hand, the Commissioner was at all times to impress upon the Chinese officials the equality and independence of the United States and to point out 'in decided terms and a positive manner' that his country could not remain on terms of friendship and regard for China if greater privileges were granted to other countries than to America. If possible he was to visit Peking and deliver in person a letter from President Tyler to the Emperor. This was one of the objects of his mission to be 'persisted in as long as may be becoming and proper.' Should he succeed, the manner of settling the problem of the kowtow was left to his discretion, but he was instructed to be careful to do nothing 'which may seem, even to the Chinese themselves, to imply any inferiority on the part of your Government.'

The tone of these instructions left little to be desired. The Commissioner was to be both firm and conciliatory. The promotion of friendly feelings with China was to be placed above any protestation of the power or dignity of the United States. Much was said about the possible visit to the court at Peking, yet it was clear that this was a secondary object. The real aim of the mission was to secure for the United States through friendly negotiation privileges for trade equal to those enjoyed by Great Britain.

Far different from the letter of instructions or Cushing's own credentials was the letter signed by President Tyler which Cushing was to present to the Son of Heaven. It was couched in such childish terms, more appropriate for an order to some petty Indian chief than for the first official communication between the President of the United States and the Emperor of China, that it seems incredible that a statesman of Webster's ability could have composed it. But the evidence is strong that, although the Secretary of State had by now resigned and been replaced by A. P. Upshur, it was his own handiwork.[1]

[1] On the controversial question of authorship of this letter, the best evidence of Webster's responsibility is a letter Cushing wrote to the State Department on June 27, 1843. He refers to 'a draft prepared by Mr. Webster of the President's letter to the Emperor of China,' and then continues: 'Please submit it to Mr. Upshur for the approval of the President and himself. It was Mr. Webster's plan to have it copied in an ornamental form and placed in a suitable box.' While Tyler Dennett seems to think that this refers to Cushing's credentials, this would not seem probable.

CALEB CUSHING IN 1843

Greeting the Emperor as 'Great and Good Friend,' this letter enumerates the names of the American States and then addresses the sovereign of a state whose civilization was old when Europe was sunk in barbarism, the heir to all the glories of Kubla Khan and those other emperors of the fabulous land of far Cathay, in these stirring words:

I hope your health is good. China is a great empire, extending over a great part of the world. The Chinese are numerous. You have millions and millions of subjects. The twenty-six United States are as large as China, though our people are not so numerous. The rising sun looks upon the great mountains and great rivers of China. When he sets, he looks upon rivers and mountains equally large in the United States. Our territories extend from one great ocean to the other; and on the west we are divided from your dominions only by the sea. Leaving the mouth of one of our great rivers, and going constantly toward the setting sun, we sail to Japan and to the Yellow sea.

Now, my words are, that the Governments of two such great countries should be at peace. It is proper, and according to the will of Heaven, that they should respect each other, and act wisely. I therefore send to your Court Caleb Cushing, one of the wise and learned men of this country. On his first arrival in China, he will inquire for your health. He has then strict orders to go to your great city of Pekin, and there to deliver this letter. He will have with him secretaries and interpreters.

The Chinese love to trade with our people, and to sell them tea and silk, for which our people pay silver, and sometimes other articles. But if the Chinese and the Americans will trade, there should be rules, so that they shall not break your laws nor our laws....

There was more of this twaddle which could not but be insulting to the Emperor, especially in its references to the trade which was so far beneath his notice, and after reference to the proposed treaty, the strange document ended with a veiled warning and the polite order: 'Let the treaty be signed by your own imperial hand. It shall be signed by mine, by the authority of our great council, the Senate.'

Equipped with his instructions, this amazing letter, and his unique collection of specimens of Western scientific invention, Commissioner Cushing was now ready to sail for China. Careful attention had been paid to the recommendations of the China merchants as to the need of some display of naval force. The squadron which was to convey our first envoy to the Empire of China was composed of four war vessels under the command of Commodore Foxhall A. Parker: the steam frigate *Missouri*, the frigate *Brandywine*, the brig *Perry*, and the sloop-of-war *St. Louis*. It was on July 31, 1843, that Cushing embarked on the expedition which was for the first time to give an official status to the trade which more than half a century earlier had been inaugurated by Samuel Shaw.

# CHAPTER XIII

## THE TREATY OF WANGHIA

THE voyage of the American mission to China was made under rather different circumstances from those which attended the voyage of the *Empress of China*. Samuel Shaw sailed to a part of the world strange and unknown to Americans; Caleb Cushing, to seas and ports which the countless voyages of his countrymen had made almost as familiar as their own coastline. And whereas in 1784 the young republic was making a first experiment in 'the adventurous pursuit of commerce,' in 1843 it was seeking a trade agreement with China as a nation which had become one of the world's commercial powers.

This contrast is still further emphasized in the fact that Cushing sailed on a steam frigate, but in this he was really anticipating the day when steam was to conquer sails. In 1843 the clipper ship was still to come into its glory and it was to be many years before steam vessels could really compete with sailing vessels. The former were regarded with much skepticism and it is probable that the members of the American mission to China fully shared this feeling. For the frigate *Missouri* had proceeded no farther on its eastward course than Gibraltar when it met disaster.

The members of the mission and the ship's officers were dining on shore when they were suddenly roused by cries in the streets of '*El vapor del frigate Americano es del fuego!*' Rushing to the harbor, they found that the *Missouri* had caught on fire while taking on coal and that the flames were already as high as her maintop. Putting out to the doomed vessel, Cushing managed to save his papers and his letters to the Chinese Emperor, but that special uniform designed to dazzle the mandarins of Canton was lost. The American envoy would not be able to appear at the council table in the full regalia of a major-general, 'with some slight additions in the way of embroideries.'

With the loss of the steam frigate, Cushing now decided to take the overland route to the East and get passage to India on a British steamer from Suez, leaving his mission to follow him on the *Brandywine* by way of the Cape of Good Hope. The two parties were then to join at Bombay. This plan worked out successfully, and after some months, during which Cushing sent home thirty voluminous reports on conditions in the various countries through which he passed, the reunited mission sailed from Bombay for China. The *Brandywine* reached Macao on February 24, 1844, and there Cushing set up 'his miniature court in the house of a former Portuguese Governor, creating a profound sensation by the novelty and magnitude of his Mission.'

Conditions in China were now calm and peaceful. The trade of both England and the United States was proceeding satisfactorily and the Chinese had informed the American merchants that they were entitled to share all the privileges which had been granted the British and that the new customs duties were to be applied to all foreigners. It was something of a question just what Cushing could hope to accomplish. The Chinese did not welcome the idea of another foreign mission and saw no need of an American treaty. The English were openly scornful and considered Cushing's embassy an idle and ridiculous ostentation. Many of the Americans even thought it a futile gesture. Their attitude was still based upon the cautious principle of letting well enough alone and doing nothing to offend the Chinese.

'When at Macao,' wrote one Canton merchant in a letter

appearing in 'Niles' Register,' 'I had the honor of seeing much of His Excellency (Cushing) who had spurs on his heels, and mustachios and imperial, very flourishing! Although I like the man, I most heartily wish he were anywhere else but here, and am, as well as every other American merchant here, in great fear. As Americans we are now on the very *best* terms possible with the Chinese; and as the only connection we want with China is a commercial one, I cannot see what Mr. Cushing expects to do. He *cannot* make us better off — and a very few of his important airs will make us hated by the Chinese, and then we lose all the advantages we now have over the English.'

Circumstances may have been inauspicious and the Chinese officials inhospitable, although forewarned by the American Consul that the mission was coming, but nevertheless Cushing was not dismayed. He knew just what he wanted to do and had planned out a careful campaign to negotiate a treaty which would guarantee for the Americans as a matter of right the privilege of trading on terms similar to those enjoyed by the British. His first act was to send to Ching, acting Governor of Canton — for the Imperial Commissioner Kiying had found it good policy to be away from Canton when the American mission arrived — a diplomatic letter inquiring for the Emperor's health and casually stating that in pursuance of his instructions he was on his way to Peking to present his credentials at the imperial court.

He did not have long to wait for a reply. The Chinese official wrote urbanely of the 'respectful obedience, and politeness exceedingly to be praised,' of the American Envoy, but he became quite agitated over the possibility of the mission proceeding to Peking. This was out of the question. 'The August Emperor, in his compassion to people from afar,' Ching dutifully informed Cushing, 'cannot bear that the Plenipotentiary, having passed the ocean, should again have the toil and trouble of traveling by land and water.'

His instructions, the Chinese official continued, were to wait the arrival of the American Envoy 'and then soothe him and stop him.' There was absolutely no need for him to seek a treaty, since one had been signed with Great Britain and 'already has your nation been bedewed with its advantages.' That was all there was to it, and Ching haughtily concluded by informing Cushing that it was 'useless with lofty, polished, and empty words to alter these unlimited advantages.'

The American knew that there was little chance of his being able to persuade the Chinese to let him proceed north, since even the English had not sent an envoy to Peking upon the signing of the Treaty of Nanking, but his instructions were to attempt to do so if it proved to be practicable. Furthermore, he clearly saw that the threat of his going despite Chinese objections might prove a useful lever to persuade the Chinese of the necessity of concluding a treaty. So he stuck to his guns. Ching was told that the question of a treaty was a matter which he could take up only with an imperial commissioner, and that in the mean time his instructions from his Government were to seek an audience with the Emperor.

The tactics of the Chinese official in this emergency were delay and procrastination. Ching now promised to memorialize the Emperor as to the proposed visit to Peking and urged Cushing to wait his answer. When the American Envoy learned that such a reply would take at least three months, he refused. He hinted quite openly that his reception in China was hardly proving to be as friendly and courteous as he had a right to expect, and ceremoniously took leave of the Chinese official.

Ching thereupon hurriedly dispatched a more conciliatory note. It would take only fifty, not ninety days, to get a reply from Peking. But Cushing was still impatient and even suggested that refusal to receive a foreign embassy might be interpreted as inviting war with other Western nations besides England. Ching unbent still further. He now declared in a letter, dwelling upon the friendliness between the United States and China, that Kiying would soon be in Canton and that he would probably be empowered by the Emperor to discuss the question of a treaty. He begged Cushing to stay until his arrival. To this the American partially assented in a final note, which again expressed his regret at Chinese inhospitality and declared that he was risking the disapprobation of his Government by submitting to any further delay.

This exchange of letters had taken almost three months, and it was not until May 8 that Cushing received a copy of an imperial edict which appointed Kiying an imperial commissioner for the negotiation of a treaty with the United States and enjoined the American mission to wait quietly at Macao 'and by no means to esteem it a light matter to agitate disorder, which is an important concern.' The long duel between the Chinese official and the American Envoy had had no apparent result other than keeping the mission in the south and forestalling the visit to Peking.

But had the victory really gone to the suave Chinese so jealously guarding his country's frontiers? In his reports to the Secretary of State, Cushing upheld the course he had followed in these preliminary negotiations in the face of severe criticism from the Americans at Canton. In the first place, he was bound by his instructions to sound out the practicality of going to Peking; in the second, his insistence upon such a course of action had enabled him to force the Chinese to appreciate the necessity of negotiating a treaty. If he had finally relinquished his right to go north, it was a sacrifice more than compensated through the attainment of the primary objective of his mission.

Furthermore, as he reported to Washington, the dilatory and futile correspondence with Ching had really cleared the way for his subsequent negotiations. It had enabled him 'to say all the harsh things which needed to be said, and to speak to the Chinese Government with extreme plainness and frankness, in a degree which would have been inconvenient, if not inadmissible, in immediate correspondence with Kiying.' When the specially appointed Commissioner took up the correspondence where Ching had left it and wrote Cushing that 'in a few days we shall take each other by the hand, and converse, and rejoice together with indescribable delight,' the American Envoy could report with good reason that the tone of this communication was the 'best possible augury for the success of the mission.'

In the midst of these first negotiations and again on the very eve of those over the proposed treaty itself, two incidents occurred which might have gravely prejudiced the incipient relations between China and the United States. The first of these was concerned with nothing more important than the weather-vane on the flagstaff in front of the American Consulate at Canton. This flagstaff had been brought out by the *Brandywine*, and its vane, in the shape of a large arrow, had been proudly set in place soon after Cushing's arrival. To the Cantonese, deeply superstitious and bitterly anti-foreign, there was something sinister about the whole affair. The city was placarded with signs declaring that the swinging arrow shot in all directions, 'thereby causing serious impediment to the felicity and good fortunes of the land.' To its mysterious influence was ascribed the serious drought which Canton was then experiencing. The resulting excitement caused a riot near the American Consulate when a Chinese mob attempted to tear the flagstaff down, and the peaceful course of Sino-American relations was saved only by the prompt removal of the charmed arrow.

The second incident was more important and its results more significant. In another of those recurrent riots which had been the expression of the increased hostility of the Cantonese toward the foreigners ever since the conclusion of the war with the British, a Chinese named Hsü A-man had been killed by an American. Governor Ching promptly demanded his surrender to the Chinese authorities.

Cushing then put into practice the most important principle which he was to embody in his treaty, that of extraterritoriality. He instructed the Consul that Americans were never to be given up to Chinese justice, and that henceforth they were to be subject to American and not to Chinese laws. Consul Forbes thereupon appointed a committee of six Americans to try the man charged with Hsü A-man's death. It considered the evidence and unanimously determined that the killing of the Chinese had been under the circumstances a justifiable act of self-defense. This decision was reported to the Chinese, and after some correspondence with Kiying, who had by then reached Canton, it was accepted as equitable and just.

In the mean time the treaty negotiations had commenced. Kiying arrived at the little Chinese village of Wanghia, just outside Macao, on June 16.[1] After an exchange of

---

[1] It is often asserted that Cushing negotiated his treaty without ever setting foot on Chinese soil. This is not true. Wanghia was outside of Portuguese jurisdiction and within Chinese territory.

courtesies, Cushing presented the Chinese Commissioner with a draft of the treaty he had in mind.

'In drawing up these minutes,' the American Envoy declared in an accompanying letter, 'I have not looked to the side of the United States alone. I felt that it would not be honorable, in dealing with Your Excellency, to take a partial view of the subject. I have inserted a multitude of provisions in the interest and for the benefit of China.'

This statement was not unwarranted, and apparently Kiying found it justified. A few modifications to the Cushing draft were mutually agreed upon, and on July 3 the treaty was signed. After the long preliminaries over whether or not there was to be a treaty, the immediate question as to its form had been settled with dispatch and address in two weeks.

On the night the treaty was signed, a banquet was held commemorative of the important event. It was a typical Chinese feast, with such delicacies as birds'-nest soup, sea-snails, seaweed, and much native wine. Cushing admitted a feeling of 'slight languor' the next day. Perhaps Kiying was not quite himself. For on receiving a copy of the famous letter for the Emperor from President Tyler, he told Cushing that he was so affected by its superlative beauty that he 'could not restrain his spirit from delight and his heart from dilating with joy.'

The relations between the two negotiators had been so friendly that the foreign community at Canton was startled some months later by the publication of what purported to be Kiying's report to the Emperor, in which the Chinese official spoke of America's 'foolish demands' and the envoy's 'stupid ignorance.' The authenticity of this document was subsequently denied by Kiying, and Cushing was later to refer to the Chinese Commissioner as 'a Manchu of high qualities of head and heart, and of perfect accomplishment.' Certainly his friendliness and understanding of the foreigners had made the course of Cushing's negotiations far smoother than he had had any right to expect. It was perhaps inevitable that Kiying should later suffer the fate of every Chinese official who had dealings with the foreigner at this period.[1] He was degraded for 'unpatriotic and pusillanimous conduct' by an edict which stated that 'at Canton he seemed only anxious to make our people serve the interest of foreigners.' Eventually he received from the Emperor a symbolic silken scarf, and duly committed suicide.

The Treaty of Wanghia not only secured for the United States all those rights and privileges which Great Britain had won in the Treaty of Nanking, with the single exception that there was no counterpart to the cession of Hongkong. It also established certain new principles for the governance of China's relations with the Western world. In subsequent years, when treaties were signed in the Far East, it was not the Treaty of Nanking which was taken as a model; it was the treaty so shrewdly negotiated by a Newburyport lawyer totally without experience in the wiles of Eastern diplomacy. Needless to say, Cushing would have faced a far different situation if the British war had not broken down the barriers of China's resistance to any political relationship with the West, or if he had not had the Treaty of Nanking on which to base his demands for American trading privileges. Nevertheless, he did not merely follow supinely in England's footsteps.

[1] The unreality with which the Chinese still continued to regard foreign relations is demonstrated by the Chinese historian of the war with England, who, in reference to the Cushing mission, wrote of the arrival of some ships from America with envoys begging to pay tribute 'and to be allowed to express their devotion at an interview.'

The two treaties differed in many important particulars.
The American instrument definitely fixed the subject of
contraband goods, specifically declared that the United
States would offer no protection to smugglers, made all
customs duties payable in cash, and left to the Chinese
authorities the responsibility of protecting American citizens in China.

Article XXXIII declared:

> Citizens of the United States who shall attempt to trade clan-
> destinely with such of the ports of China as are not open to foreign
> commerce, or who shall trade in opium or any other contraband
> articles of merchandise, shall be subject to be dealt with by the
> Chinese Government without being entitled to any countenance
> or protection from that of the United States; and the United
> States will take measures to prevent their flag from being abused
> by the subjects of other nations as a cover for the violation of the
> laws of the Empire.

The effect of these measures was to throw upon China the
entire responsibility of enforcing its own customs regulations, while the British treaty had left the collection of
customs duties in the hands of British consuls and had
omitted all reference to the critical question of opium. In
his discussion of the British and American treaties, Tyler
Dennett has stated that in this divergence of policy, the
English treaties, aside from the opium question, were more
beneficent to China than the Treaty of Wanghia, although
the latter may have been more benevolent. He has also
said that in regard to smuggling the treaties had in practice
the same effect. Both these statements are justified by the
way things worked out in the course of the next few years,
but at the time the treaties were signed, their full effect
could not have been foreseen. The fundamental difference
in 1844 on these points was that Great Britain was following

her traditional policy in the East of providing for British protection of all British interests, while the United States was treating China more as an equal and asserting a Chinese obligation to handle all relations with foreigners and to guard their interests.

The American treaty also had several provisions which were in effect an extension of the privileges the English had secured and Great Britain was to take advantage of these as quickly as the United States had taken advantage of the provisions of the British treaty. They included the right to enjoy all proper accommodation in hiring sites from the inhabitants, not only for the construction of houses and places of business, but also for hospitals, churches, and cemeteries; the privilege of employing scholars to teach Chinese and of purchasing all manner of books; the right of merchant ships to remain in port forty-eight hours without paying duties, or, if they had paid duties, to reëxport their cargo without further charges and visit other ports; and, finally, a stipulation for the revision of the treaty after twelve years.

The most important articles in the Treaty of Wanghia, however, are still to be mentioned. It was Caleb Cushing who definitely established the principle of extraterritoriality in the relations between China and the West and asserted in specific terms the independence of American citizens from China's legal jurisdiction.

The British had for long recognized the need of extraterritoriality because of the peculiar nature of Chinese criminal law, and there is no question but that China's concession of this privilege was one of the fruits of the Anglo-Chinese War. But in Hongkong the British had secured a means to exercise territorial jurisdiction of their own which made it unnecessary for them to insist upon a concise acknowledgment of their rights in either of their treaties. The Americans, however, had no equivalent for Hongkong, and Cushing felt it absolutely necessary to secure from the Chinese a precise definition of the status of American citizens in relation to Chinese law which would give permanence to the principle he had already practiced in his refusal to hand over to Chinese justice the American charged with the death of Hsü A-man.

This he did in the following two articles of his treaty, which were subsequently adopted in substance by all other Western nations having treaty relations with China:

Article XXI. Subjects of China who may be guilty of any criminal act towards the citizens of the United States shall be arrested and punished by the Chinese authorities according to the laws of China; and citizens of the United States who may commit any crime in China shall be subject to be tried and punished only by the Consul, or other public functionary of the United States, thereto authorized, according to the laws of the United States....

Article XXV. All questions in regard to rights, whether of property or person, arising between citizens of the United States in China, shall be subject to the jurisdiction of, and regulated by the authorities of their own Government. And all controversies occurring in China between the citizens of the United States and the subjects of any other Government shall be regulated by the treaties existing between the United States and such Governments, respectively, without interference on the part of China.

Cushing made his attainment of absolute and unqualified extraterritoriality the subject of a long and ably argued dispatch to Secretary of State John C. Calhoun. The precedent on which he sought this right was found in the special privileges exercised by foreign consuls in such non-Christian countries as the Barbary States and Turkey. He argued that China, for all its civilization, was in the same category

as these States, since it was not within the Christian family
of nations and neither understood nor accepted those
principles of international law which governed the relations
of the countries of the West.

He recognized that the concession of extraterritoriality
might be unwise for the states of Asia and Africa, but declared that it would be 'time enough for them to claim
jurisdiction over Christian foreigners, when these last can
visit Mecca, Damascus, Fez, or Peking, as safely and freely
as they do Rome and Paris, and when submission to the
local jurisdiction becomes *reciprocal*.' It was not his idea to
attack Chinese sovereignty, but to provide a means to avoid
the disputes which would inevitably arise, as in the Terranova case, if the Americans were subject to Chinese jurisdiction, while the English could avoid it by recourse to their
own courts in Hongkong.

In 1844, extraterritoriality was virtually necessary for the
friendly development of foreign trade in China, and the
Chinese authorities seem to have recognized this as clearly
as the foreigners once their original haughty disregard of all
foreign rights had become modified. It was the only solution of the difficult problem offered by the divergent ideas of
the East and the West in all matters of law and justice.
If only at the time of its incorporation into the foreign
treaties some provision had been inserted declaring that
extraterritoriality was a temporary expedient to meet an
existing emergency, and that the privileges it conferred
would be surrendered when Chinese law was brought more
in harmony with Western law, much subsequent friction and
Chinese hostility might have been avoided.

In all events the Treaty of Wanghia represented a fair and
equitable adjustment of the problems inherent in Sino-
American relations of that period. In relation to the

treaties already signed by Great Britain, it was as much to the advantage of the Chinese in protecting them from any undue British influence, as it was to the advantage of the United States in preventing its trade rivals from securing a most-favored-nation position in the Far East.

Its prompt ratification by the Emperor, who declared that its terms were 'all perspicuous, and entirely and perfectly judicious, and forever worthy of adherence,' and its unanimous approval by the United States Senate offer striking evidence of the light in which it was officially viewed in China and America. As for the opinion of the British on what Cushing had accomplished, R. Montgomery Martin, an authoritative writer on things Chinese, declared that 'the United States Government in their treaty with China, and in vigilant protection of their subjects at Canton, have evinced far better diplomacy, and more attention to substantial interests, than we have done, although it has not cost them as many groats as we have spent guineas, while their position in China is really more advantageous than that of England, after our own sacrifices of blood and treasure.'

If the treaties first negotiated by England, then by the United States, and a little later by France, opened up China to the Western world and first asserted the principle of international equality in the relations between China and the foreign powers, they also meant one other thing. They spelled the end of an era. The period of those hazardous voyages which had opened up the China trade for the adventurous merchants and seamen of the United States had been drawing to a close with the development of a more substantial and regular commerce. The treaties marked the culmination of this gradual change.

For sixty years the American trade had prospered without

benefit of diplomacy; now it was to be aided and protected by a treaty. The future held out tremendous possibilities. But among those remaining pioneers of the early days of the China trade there were some few who realized with regret that for all the benefits the treaties conferred they were 'the "knell, the shroud, the mattock, and the grave" of old Canton.'

THE END

# APPENDIX

No complete statistics covering the China trade from 1784 to 1844 are available. In the following table the number of American ships employed at Canton and the quantities of tea exported for the period 1784–85 to 1803–04 are taken from William Milburn's *Oriental Commerce* (London, 1813), and for 1804–05 to 1819–20, from estimates of the Senate Finance Committee as reported in House Document 137, nineteenth Congress, first session. There are no figures for American exports and imports for the first of these two periods. For the second, their annual values, as of Canton, are taken from the Senate Finance Committee's report. From 1821 on official figures are available in U.S. Treasury reports giving American exports to China and imports from China. They may be found for almost the entire period (together with the number of the American ships which sailed to the United States from Canton) in House Document 35, twenty-seventh Congress, third session. Various other statistical tables (incomplete) appear in other sources, while an almost similar tabulation may be found in Kenneth Scott Latourette's *Voyages of American Ships to China, 1784–1844*, in *Transactions of the Connecticut Academy of Arts and Sciences*, vol. 28. New Haven, 1927.

## TABLE OF AMERICAN TRADE WITH CHINA, 1784–1844

| YEAR | IMPORTS AT CANTON FROM UNITED STATES | EXPORTS FROM CANTON TO UNITED STATES | SHIPS IN THE TRADE | TEA EXPORTS TO UNITED STATES (pounds) |
|---|---|---|---|---|
| 1784–1785......... | | | 2 | 880,100 |
| 1785–1786......... | | | 1 | 695,000 |
| 1786–1787......... | | | 5 | 1,181,860 |
| 1787–1788......... | | | 2 | 750,000 |
| 1788–1789......... | | | 4 | 1,188,800 |
| 1789–1790......... | | | 14 | 3,093,200 |
| 1790–1791......... | | | 3 | 743,100 |
| 1791–1792......... | | | 3 | 1,863,200 |
| 1792–1793......... | | | 6 | 1,538,400 |
| 1793–1794......... | | | 7 | 1,974,130 |
| 1794–1795......... | | | 7 | 1,438,270 |
| 1795–1796......... | | | 10 | 2,819,600 |
| 1796–1797......... | | | 13 | 3,450,400 |
| 1797–1798......... | | | 10 | 3,100,400 |
| 1798–1799......... | | | 13 | 5,674,000 |
| 1799–1800......... | | | 18 | 5,665,067 |
| 1800–1801......... | | | 23 | 4,762,866 |
| 1801–1802......... | | | 31 | 5,740,734 |
| 1802–1803......... | | | 20 | 2,612,436 |
| 1803–1804......... | | | 13 | 2,371,600 |
| 1804–1805......... | $3,555,818 | $3,842,000 | 34 | 7,679,120 |
| 1805–1806......... | 5,326,358 | 5,127,000 | 42 | 9,830,480 |
| 1806–1807......... | 3,877,362 | 4,294,000 | 37 | 9,402,160 |
| 1807–1808......... | 3,940,090 | 3,476,000 | 33 | 5,654,480 |
| 1808–1809......... | 479,850 | 808,000 | 8 | 1,562,320 |
| 1809–1810......... | 5,744,600 | 5,715,000 | 37 | 9,224,880 |
| 1810–1811......... | 2,898,800 | 2,973,000 | 16 | 2,615,520 |
| 1811–1812......... | 3,132,810 | 2,771,000 | 25 | 3,496,880 |
| 1812–1813......... | 1,453,000 | 620,000 | 8 | 1,436,800 |
| ................. | | | ...... | |
| 1813–1815......... | 451,500 | 572,000 | 9 | 1,469,360 |
| 1815–1816......... | 2,527,500 | 4,220,000 | 30 | 7,723,200 |
| 1816–1817......... | 5,609,600 | 5,703,000 | 38 | 9,391,680 |
| 1817–1818......... | 7,076,828 | 6,777,000 | 39 | 9,701,040 |
| 1818–1819......... | 9,876,208 | 9,057,000 | 47 | 12,035,280 |
| 1819–1820......... | 8,185,800 | 8,173,000 | 43 | 10,519,160 |
| 1820–1821......... | 4,290,560 | 3,111,951 | 15 | 4,973,463 |
| 1821–1822......... | 5,935,368 | 5,242,536 | 26 | 6,636,705 |
| 1822–1823......... | 4,636,061 | 6,511,425 | 35 | 8,208,895 |
| 1823–1824......... | 5,301,171 | 5,618,502 | 28 | 8,919,210 |
| 1824–1825......... | 5,570,515 | 7,533,115 | 36 | 10,178,972 |
| 1825–1826......... | 2,566,644 | 7,422,186 | 28 | 10,072,898 |
| 1826–1827......... | 3,864,405 | 3,617,183 | 24 | 5,868,828 |
| 1827–1828......... | 1,482,802 | 5,339,108 | 27 | 7,689,305 |
| 1828–1829......... | 1,354,862 | 4,680,847 | 22 | 6,595,033 |
| 1829–1830......... | 742,193 | 3,878,141 | 23 | 8,584,799 |

## AMERICAN TRADE WITH CHINA, 1784–1844, *continued.*

| Year | Imports at Canton from United States | Exports from Canton to United States | Ships in the Trade | Tea Exports to United States (pounds) |
|------|------|------|------|------|
| 1830–1831.......... | 1,290,835 | 3,083,205 | 11 | 5,177,557 |
| 1831–1832.......... | 1,580,522 | 5,344,907 | 30 | 9,894,181 |
| 1832–1833.......... | 1,433,759 | 7,541,570 | 41 | 14,637,486 |
| 1833–1834.......... | 1,010,483 | 7,892,327 | 43 | 16,267,852 |
| 1834–1835.......... | 1,868,580 | 5,987,187 | 36 | 14,403,458 |
| 1835–1836.......... | 1,194,264 | 7,324,816 | 43 | 16,347,344 |
| 1836–1837.......... | 600,591 | 8,965,337 | 42 | 16,942,122 |
| 1837–1838.......... | 1,516,602 | 4,764,536 | 29 | 14,411,337 |
| 1838–1839.......... | 1,533,601 | 3,678,509 | 18 | 9,296,679 |
| 1839–1840.......... | 1,009,966 | 6,640,829 | 35 | |
| 1840–1841.......... | 1,200,816 | 3,985,388 | 28 | |
| 1841–1842.......... | 1,444,397 | 4,934,645 | | |
| 1842–1843.......... | 2,418,958 | 4,385,566 | | |
| 1843–1844.......... | 1,756,941 | 4,931,255 | | |

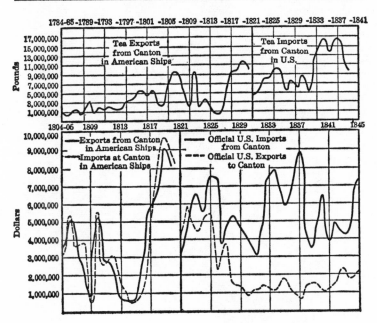

# SOURCES

Abeel, David: *Journal of a Residence in China*. New York, 1836.

Alexander, W. D.: *Account Books of William French, 1818–19*. Papers of Hawaiian Historical Society, No. 11, 1904.

America and England: Bancroft Collection MSS., New York Public Library.

American State Papers: *Finance*, vol. 1; *Commerce and Navigation*, vols. 1 and 2. Washington, 1832.

Appleton, Nathaniel: *Journal on Board Ship Concord, 1799–1802*. MSS., Essex Institute.

Auber, Peter: *China: an Outline of the Government, Laws and Policy*. London, 1834.

Backhouse, E., and Bland, J. O. P.: *Annals and Memoirs of the Court of Peking*. London, 1914.

Bancroft, Hubert Howe: *History of the Pacific States of North America*, vol. 14 (California) and vols. 22 and 23 (The Northwest Coast). San Francisco, 1882–90.

Barnard, Captain Charles H.: *A Narrative of the Sufferings and Adventures of*. New York, 1829.

Barrett, Walter (Joseph A. Scoville): *The Old Merchants of New York City*. 4 vols. New York, 1863–66.

Barrow, Sir John: *Travels in China*. London, 1804.

Bartlett, John: *Remarks on Board the Ship Massachusetts, 1790*. MSS., Peabody Museum.

Benton, Thomas H.: *Abridgement of the Debates of Congress, from 1789 to 1856*, vols. 7, 8, 10. New York, 1858.

Benton, Thomas H.: *Thirty Years' View*. 2 vols. New York, 1861–62.

Boit, John, Jr.: 'Remarks on the Ship *Columbia's* Voyage from Boston (1790–92).' *Proceedings*, Massachusetts Historical Society, vol. 53, 1920; and *Washington Historical Quarterly*, vol. 12, 1921.

Bond, Phineas, Letters of: *American Historical Association Reports*, vol. 1, 1896. Washington, 1897.

Callahan, James Morton: *American Relations in the Pacific and the Far East, 1784–1900*. Johns Hopkins University Studies in Historical and Political Science, Series 19, Nos. 1–3. Baltimore, 1901.

Campbell, Archibald: *A Voyage Around the World, from 1806 to 1812*. Edinburgh, 1816.

Cary, Thomas G.: *Memoir of Thomas Handasyd Perkins*. Boston, 1856.

*Chinese Repository, The*. Vols. 1–20. Canton, 1832–51.

Clark, A. Howard: 'The Antarctic Fur-Seal and Sea-Elephant Industry'; in section 5, vol. 2, *The Fisheries and Fishery Industries of the United States*, by George Brown Goode. Washington, 1887.

Clark, Arthur H.: *The Clipper Ship Era*. New York and London, 1910.

Cleland, Robert G.: *Asiatic Trade and the American Occupation of the Pacific Coast*. American Historical Association Reports, vol. 1, 1914. Washington, 1916.

Cleveland, H. W. S.: *Voyages of a Merchant Navigator*. New York, 1886.

Cleveland, Richard J.: *A Narrative of Voyages and Commercial Enterprises*. 2 vols. Cambridge, 1842.

*Congressional Globe*.

Cordier, Henri: *Americains et Français à Canton au XVIIIᵉ Siècle*. Journal de la Société des Americanistes de Paris, 1898.

Cordier, Henri: *Histoire générale de la Chine et de ses relations avec les pays étrangères*. 4 vols. Paris, 1920.

Corney, Peter: *Voyages in the Northern Pacific*. Honolulu, 1896.

Couling, Samuel: *Encyclopædia Sinica*. Shanghai, 1917.

Coxe, Tench: *A View of the United States of America*. Philadelphia, 1794.

Davis, John Francis: *China, during the War and since the Peace*. 2 vols. London, 1852.

Davis, John Francis: *Sketches of China*. 2 vols. London, 1841.

Davis, John Francis: *The Chinese*. 2 vols. London, 1836.

Delano, Amasa: *Narrative of Voyages and Travels in the Northern and Southern Hemispheres*. Boston, 1817.

Dennett, Tyler: *Americans in Eastern Asia*. New York, 1922.

Downing, C. Toogood: *The Fan-Qui in China in 1836–37*. 3 vols. London, 1838.

D'Wolf, Captain John: *A Voyage to the North Pacific*. Cambridge, 1861.

Eames, James Bromley: *The English in China*. London, 1909.

Eitel, E. J.: *Europe in China*. London and Hongkong, 1895.

*Experiment, Papers Relating to the Voyage of the Sloop, 1785–87*. MSS., New York Historical Society.

Fanning, Captain Edmund: *Voyages Round the World*. New York, 1833. Also under title: *Voyages and Discoveries in the South Seas, 1792–1832*. Marine Research Society, Salem, 1924.

Fanning, Captain Edmund: *Voyages to the South Seas, Indian and Pacific Oceans*. New York, 1838.

Forbes, John Murray: *Letters and Recollections*. 2 vols. Boston, 1899.

Forbes, Robert B.: *Notes on Navigation*. Boston, 1884.

Forbes, Robert B.: *Personal Reminiscences*. Boston, 1878.

Forbes, Robert B.: *Remarks on China and the China Trade*. Boston, 1844.

Foster, John W.: *American Diplomacy in the Orient*. Boston and New York, 1904.

Franchère, Gabriel: *Narrative of a Voyage to the Northwest Coast of America*. New York, 1854.

Fuess, Claude M.: *The Life of Caleb Cushing*. 2 vols. New York, 1923.

Great Britain — Parliament: *Sessional Papers*. Vol. 7, 1821; vols. 5 and 6, 1830; vol. 36, 1840; and vol. 40, 1847.

Greenbie, Sydney and Marjorie: *Gold of Ophir*. New York, 1925.

Greenhow, Robert: *The History of Oregon and California*. Boston, 1845.

Grimes, Captain Eliah: 'Letters on Northwest Fur Trade'; in *Washington Historical Quarterly*, vol. 11, 1920.

Guthrie, William: *A New Geographical, Historical, and Commercial Grammar*. Edinburgh, 1807.

Gutzlaff, Reverend Charles: *A Sketch of Chinese History*. 2 vols. London, 1834.

Gutzlaff, Reverend Charles: *Journal of Three Voyages Along the Coast of China*. London, 1840.

Haswell, Robert: 'A Voyage Round the World on Board the Ship *Columbia Rediviva* and Sloop *Washington* in 1787–89'; in Appendix of H. H. Bancroft's *History of the Northwest Coast*, vol. 1. San Francisco, 1886.

Hill, Hamilton Andrews: 'Trade, Commerce and Navigation of Boston, 1780–1880'; in *Memorial History of Boston*, ed. Justin Winsor. 4 vols. Boston, 1881.

Hill, Samuel: *Autobiography*. MSS., New York Public Library.

Hill, Samuel: *Journal and Log of the Ophelia and Packet*. MSS., New York Public Library.

Howay, F. W.: 'Letters Relating to the Second Voyage of the *Columbia*'; in *Quarterly of Oregon Historical Society*, vol. 24, 1923.

Howay, F. W.: 'The Voyage of the *Hope*: 1790–92'; in *Washington Historical Quarterly*, vol. 11, 1920.

*Hudson Collection of Papers Relating to Ship Massachusetts*. MSS., New York Public Library.

Hunt, Freeman: *Lives of American Merchants*. 2 vols. New York, 1856.

Hunter, William C.: *Bits of Old China*. Shanghai, 1911.

Hunter, William C.: *The 'Fan Kwae' at Canton*. London, 1882.

Ingraham, Joseph: *The Log of the Brig Hope*. Hawaiian Historical Society Reprint, No. 3.

Irving, Washington: *Astoria*. 3 vols. London, 1836.

Jacobs, Thomas Jefferson: *Scenes, Incidents and Adventures in the Pacific Ocean*. New York, 1844.

Jewitt, John R.: *A Narrative of the Adventures and Sufferings of*. Middletown, Conn., 1815.

Johnson, Emory R. and others: *History of Domestic and Foreign Commerce of the United States*. 2 vols. Washington, 1915.

'Journal of a Voyage Between China and the North-Western Coast of America'; in *The American Register: or, General Repository of History, Politics and Science*, vol. 3. Philadelphia, 1808.

Kimball, Gertrude Selwyn: *The East India Trade of Providence from 1787 to 1807*. Brown University Papers from the Historical Seminary, No. 6. 1896.

Krusenstern, A. J. von: *Voyage Round the World in 1803–06*. 2 vols. London, 1813.

Latourette, Kenneth Scott: 'The History of Early Relations Between the United States and China, 1784–1844'; in *Transactions of the Connecticut Academy of Arts and Sciences*, vol. 22. New Haven, 1917.

Latourette, Kenneth Scott: 'Voyages of American Ships to China, 1784–1844'; in *Transactions of the Connecticut Academy of Arts and Sciences*, vol. 28. New Haven, 1927.

Law, William: Papers of, 1808–17. MSS., New York Public Library.

Ledyard, John: *A Journal of Captain Cook's Last Voyage to the Pacific Ocean*. Hartford, 1783.

Lockerby, William: *The Journal of*. Hakluyt Society, Second Series, vol. 52. London, 1925.

Loring, Charles G.: *Memoir of William Sturgis*. Boston, 1864.

Low, Charles P.: *Some Recollections*. Boston, 1905.

Low, Miss Harriet: *My Mother's Journal*. Ed. Katherine Hillard. Boston, 1900.

MacNair, Harley Farnsworth: *Modern Chinese History: Selected Readings*. Shanghai, 1923.

Macpherson, David: *Annals of Commerce*, vol. 4. London, 1805.

Magee, Bernard: *Observations on the Islands of Juan Fernandez*, etc. Collections of the Massachusetts Historical Society, vol. 4, 1795.

Magee, Captain James: *An Account of a Discovery of a Group of Islands*. Collections of the Massachusetts Historical Society, vol. 4, 1795.

*Margaret, Extracts from the Log of Ship*, 1792. MSS., Essex Institute.

Martin, R. Montgomery: *British Relations with the Chinese Empire*. London, 1832.

Martin, R. Montgomery: *China: Political, Commercial, and Social*. 2 vols. London, 1847.

Marvin, Winthrop L.: *The American Merchant Marine*. New York, 1902.

*Merchants' Magazine, The* (Hunt's), vols. 1–14. New York, 1839–46.

Milburn, William: *Oriental Commerce*. 2 vols. London, 1813.

Molineux, F.: *Receipts — Canton in China, October 8th, 1784*. MSS., private possession.

Morison, Samuel Eliot: 'Boston Traders in the Hawaiian Islands, 1789–1823'; in *Washington Historical Quarterly*, vol. 12, 1921.

Morison, Samuel Eliot: *Maritime History of Massachusetts*. Boston and New York, 1925.

Morrell, Benjamin: *A Narrative of Four Voyages*. New York, 1832.

Morrison, John Robert: *A Chinese Commercial Guide*. Canton, 1834.

Morrison, Robert: *Memoirs of the Life and Labors of*. Compiled by his Widow. 2 vols. London, 1839.

Morse, Hosea Ballou, and MacNair, Harley Farnsworth: *Far Eastern International Relations*. Shanghai, 1928.

Morse, Hosea Ballou: *The Chronicles of the East India Company Trading to China, 1635–1834*. 4 vols. Oxford, 1926.

Morse, Hosea Ballou: *The International Relations of the Chinese Empire*. Vol. 1, 'The Period of Conflict, 1834–1860.' London, 1910.

Morse, Hosea Ballou: *Trade and Administration of the Chinese Empire*. New York, Bombay, and Calcutta, 1908.

Moulton, William: *A Concise Extract, from the Sea Journal of*. Utica, 1804.

*Niles' Weekly Register*. Baltimore, 1811–49.

*North American Review*, vol. 40. 1835.

Nye, Gideon, Jr.: *The Morning of my Life in China*. Canton, 1873.

Nye, Gideon, Jr.: *Peking the Goal*. Canton, 1873.

Nye, Gideon, Jr.: *Tea: and the Tea Trade*. New York, 1850.

Oberholtzer, Ellis Paxson: *Robert Morris*. New York, 1903.

Oliver, James: *Wreck of the Glide*. New York, 1848.

Osgood, Charles S., and Batcheldeŕ, H. M.: *Historical Sketch of Salem*. Salem, 1879.

Paine, Ralph D.: *The Ships and Sailors of Old Salem*. New York, 1909.

Parker, E. H.: *China's Intercourse with Europe*. Pagoda Library, No. 2. Shanghai, 1890.

Parker, E. H.: *Chinese Account of the Opium War*. Pagoda Library, No. 1. Shanghai, 1888.

Patterson, Samuel: *Narrative of Adventures and Sufferings of*. Palmer, Mass., 1817.

Paullin, Charles Oscar: *Diplomatic Negotiations of American Naval Officers, 1778–1883*. Baltimore, 1912.

Paullin, Charles Oscar: 'Early Voyages of American Naval Vessels to the Orient,' in *Proceedings of United States Naval Institute*, vol. 36. Annapolis, 1910.

Peabody, Robert E.: *Merchant Venturers of Old Salem*. Boston, 1912.

Peabody, Robert E.: *The Log of the Grand Turk*. Boston, 1926.

Phipps, John: *A Practical Treatise on the China and the Eastern Trade*. Calcutta, 1835.

Pitkin, Timothy: *A Statistical View of the Commerce of the United States of America.* Hartford, 1816 and (additional material) New Haven, 1835.

Porter, David: *Journal of a Cruise Made to the Pacific Ocean.* 2 vols. New York, 1822.

Porter, Edward G.: *The Discovery of the Columbia River.* Old South Leaflets, No. 131, Boston, and *New England Magazine,* vol. 6, 1892.

*Press, The Canton.* Vol. 1, No. 39, 1836.

Putnam, George Granville: *Salem Vessels and Their Voyages.* Salem, 1925.

Roberts, Edmund: *Embassy to the Eastern Courts.* New York, 1837.

Root, Joel: *Narrative of a Sealing and Trading Voyage in the Ship Huron.* New Haven Colony Historical Society Papers, vol. 5. 1894.

Ross, Alexander: *Adventures of the First Settlers on the Oregon or Columbia River.* London, 1849.

Ruschenberger, W. S. W.: *A Voyage Round the World.* Philadelphia, 1838.

Scharf, J. Thomas, and Westcott, Thompson: *History of Philadelphia.* Philadelphia, 1884.

*Sea, the Ship and the Sailor, The.* Marine Research Society. Salem, 1925.

Seybert, Adam: *Statistical Annals of the United States.* 2 vols. Philadelphia, 1818.

Shaw, Major Samuel: *The Journals of.* Edited, with a life of the author, by Joseph Quincy. Boston, 1847.

Sheffield, Lord: *Observations on the Commerce of the American States.* London, 1783.

Smith, Arthur D. Howden: *John Jacob Astor.* Philadelphia, 1929.

Sparks, Jared: *The Life of John Ledyard.* Cambridge, 1828.

Spears, John R.: *Captain Nathaniel Brown Palmer.* New York, 1922.

Spears, John R.: *The Story of the American Merchant Marine.* New York, 1910.

Speer, William: *The Oldest and the Newest Empire: China and the United States.* Pittsburgh, 1877.

Staunton, Sir George L.: *An Authentic Account of an Embassy from the King of Great Britain to the Emperor of China.* 2 vols. London, 1797.

Staunton, Sir George Thomas: *Miscellaneous Notices Relating to China.* London, 1850.

Stevens, John Austin: *Progress of New York in a Century, 1776–1876.* New York, 1876.

Stewart, C. S.: *Journal of a Residence in the Sandwich Islands.* 2 vols. New York, 1828.

Sturgis, William: *The Northwest Fur Trade.* Old South Leaflets, No. 219. Boston.

Swan, James G.: *The Northwest Coast.* New York, 1857.

Taylor, Fitch W.: *A Voyage Round the World.* New Haven, 1855.

Townsend, Mr. Ebenezer, Jr.: *The Diary of.* New Haven Colony Historical Society Papers, vol. 4, 1888.

*Treaties, Conventions, International Acts, Protocols and Agreements between the United States of America and Other Powers, 1776–1909.* Comp. William M. Malloy. 2 vols. Washington, 1910.

Trowbridge, Thomas Rutherford, Jr.: *History of the Ancient Maritime Interests of New Haven.* New Haven Colony Historical Society Papers, vol. 3, 1882.

United States: *Diplomatic Correspondence, 1783–89.* Vol. 3. Washington, 1834.

United States: *House Documents.* 19th Congress, 1st Session, No. 137; 26th Congress, 1st Session, Nos. 40, 57, 119, 170, and 248; 26th Congress, 2d Session, Nos. 34 and 71; 27th Congress, 3d Session, No. 35.

United States: *Senate Documents.* 19th Congress, 1st Session, No. 31; 28th Congress, 2d Session, Nos. 58, 67, and 138; 29th Congress, 1st Session, No. 139.

Williams, S. Wells: 'Establishment of American Trade at Canton'; in *China Review,* vol. 5. Hongkong, 1876.

Williams, S. Wells: *Recollections of China Prior to 1840.* Journal of North-China Branch of Royal Asiatic Society, New Series, No. 8. Shanghai, 1874.

Williams, S. Wells: *The Middle Kingdom.* 2 vols. New York, 1901.

Wines, E. C.: *A Peep at China.* Philadelphia, 1839.

Wolcott, Oliver: *Account Book,* New York, 1804–10. MSS., New York Historical Society.

Wood, W. W.: *Sketches of China.* Philadelphia, 1830.

# INDEX

# INDEX